Tanks on stamps

Christopher B Yardley PhD

Counties of issue – in alphabetical order

A Cannava House Publication
Canberra, Australian Capital Territory
Cannava@iinet.net.au

National Library of Australia
Cataloguing-in-Publication entry
Yardley, Christopher B.
Tanks on stamps
ISBN : 978-0-6486671-3-1
EPub ISBN : 978-0-6486671-4-8

Keywords :
i)	First World War
ii)	Second World War.
iii)	World Wars.
iii)	Postage stamps 1914-2024.
iv)	History of human conflict 1914-2024.
v)	Military History on postage stamps.
vi)	Tanks on postage stamps

Cover image : A first day cover from Royal Mail with a set of stamps issued in Britain 2021 : "British Army vehicles".

Back cover image : Two miniature sheets from the Central African Republic 2019 "The 75th Anniversary of the Battle of Bulge".

Preface

The devil's in the detail, they say. And as far as the miniscule art form of stamp design is concerned, this couldn't be more true. The amount of contemplation and concentration involved in creating such a diminutive image is sizeable. Every pixel counts, every micro-millimetre needs to do its bit.

But of course, a stamp can only say so much. It's an impression, a small window to people and stories and celebrations, a cue to find out more.

By presenting (these) diverse subjects in summary and in detail, we hope to give you a fresh perspective. After all, our stamps may be small, but their scope and ambition are enormous (Editorial (2010), "The big picture", Royal Mail Yearbook).

Why have I examined "Tanks on stamps"?

I have previously published four reference books that have looked at the postage stamps commemorating the First World War, the second World War (2 volumes) and companion volume on the Other Wars of the Twentieth Century.

The more I look into how the world's postal authorities look at history (on the date that they issue a postage stamp for general use by the public) they are describing the history of an event as viewed on the date of issue. The images carry the name of the country as a sign of the integrity of the image and the story it tells. Some countries will, of course, pursue their political and propaganda objectives through the image and stories they are telling. But it is still history in most cases, a "changing history" published because the issuing authority has decided to publish that message.

Sources for the stamps I have reproduced in this review

I have used my own collection as much as I can. I choose to only collect, when available, stamps that have fulfilled their niche role and have been used to carry mail. The postal authority has officially cancelled these stamps with, hopefully, a circular date-stamp showing the entry point into the system and that date of posting. Occasionally this 'spoils' the image, but not often. I have chosen to use the sharpest image that I have when scanning my own stamps.

I have made extensive use of stamp catalogues to garner appropriate representations of battles / conflicts and confirm I am not missing any images, where I can. Catalogues come in printed form and / or in digital form via the Internet.

On a world-wide basis four catalogues are used as 'bibles', these are :

1. Michel: Deutschland, Europa and Überseekatalog
2. Scott: Standard Postage Stamp Catalog
3. Stanley Gibbons: Stamps of the World
4. Yvert & Tellier: Catalogue de Timbres-Poste

Where necessary I have used the digital images of the *Stampworld* catalogue, the Postal Authorities own websites and commercial sales outlets, such as *e-bay*, to find the appropriate image I was looking for.

Tanks on stamps

When is a stamp NOT a stamp?

Four independent stamp agencies, plus a few other organisations, on contract take care of the designing, manufacturing, issuing, marketing and selling of postage stamps on behalf of a country's postal administration. In this study we shall come across the activities of :

> The Inter-Governmental Philatelic Corporation (IGPC) of New York,
> Impressor SA based in Syens, Switzerland,
> Unicover Corporation of Wyoming, USA and
> Stamperija Limited of Vilnius, Lithuania.

These companies have a style that is their own and recognisable to a collector. For each subject selected to provide the excuse to print a set of stamps they will generally issue four stamps, (within a miniature sheet) and a higher value stamp also within a miniature sheet. The subjects offered are those that the design-agency believes will sell the most copies. These pseudo-stamps look like stamps and are available to the collector, not necessarily from the country's post offices but commercially, and not necessarily for the implied service-fee. However :

> The Universal Postal Union (UPU) in 2016 published a revised
> Philatelic Code of Ethics for the use of UPU members when issuing
> and supplying postage stamps and other philatelic products.
>
> According to it when choosing themes and other design elements
> the issuing postal authorities *shall not produce postage stamps or
> philatelic products that are intended to exploit customers.* In other
> words issuing postal authorities shall not produce any abusive
> issues.
> (www.fitphitalelicphilately.org/2020/TCNewsNo29 September2020)

I have not included abusive issues. To my mind the postal authority has commissioned designs to meet issue criteria (subject and time requirements) and have then chosen the design that best suits their needs. The designer has had access to data required for him to contextualise the subject as it is regarded at the time of design / issue. This up-to-date research creating living history. I am therefore inclined to not use the description 'pseudo-stamps' – they are images of a changing perspective of historical events.

Sending mail

All postal authorities are confronted with a diminishing market.[1]

The Internet has reduced the sending of mail by as much as 80%. Automation of the post office means that the clerk will more readily print a label to show the service fee to be paid for carriage of an article rather than tear a stamp from a printed sheet. Very little of the posted mail I receive these days has a stamp on the envelope.

85% of all stamps sold are to collectors.

The clerk in today's post office is not interested in selling a single stamp and the product, remembering that it is the collector who is buying, is made available in many attractive formats. Many of these formats show the context of the issue to attract the casual buyer, souvenir hunter. The clerk has been encouraged to sell multiple stamps via stamp booklets, prestige stamp booklets and or within miniature sheets where the service fees cover the same or multiple service options.

Points of inflection

The term "point of inflection" is often used to describe a significant turning point in military history. It refers to a moment when a fundamental change occurs in the character of war, which can have a profound impact on the outcome of a conflict.
One example of a point of inflection in military history is the development of the tank during World War I. The introduction of this new technology fundamentally changed the way wars were fought, and it had a significant impact on the outcome of the conflict.
Another example is the development of nuclear weapons during World War II. This technology fundamentally changed the nature of warfare and had a profound impact on international relations and global security.
It is important to note that points of inflection are not always related to technological advancements. They can also be related to changes in strategy, tactics, or doctrine. For example, the development of Blitzkrieg tactics by the Germans during World War II was a significant point of inflection in military history.

In summary, points of inflection in military history refer to significant turning points that fundamentally change the character of war. They can be related to

---

[1] Reality and author's observation and research.

technological advancements, changes in strategy, tactics, or doctrine, and they can have a profound impact on the outcome of a conflict (Downloaded through Microsoft Bing, from the Internet 15.i.24).

Changing Character of War

The rapid change in the character of war demands a corresponding fundamental shift in our Joint Force. As Carl von Clausewitz stated, the *nature* of war—a violent contest of wills to achieve political aims—is immutable. Humans will continue to impose their political will on opponents with violence. Clausewitz also tells us the nature of war involves fear, friction, uncertainty, and chance inherent in the dynamic interaction among the government, the people, and the military.

However, the *character* of war—how, where, with what weapons, and technologies wars are fought—is changing rapidly. For example, the last fundamental change in the character of war occurred between World War I and World War II. Technological advancements fundamentally transformed the character of warfare: mechanization and the use of wheeled and tracked vehicles; widespread employment of the aircraft, including development of bombers and fighters; and proliferation of radio to coordinate and synchronize dispersed units. The way militaries conducted warfare—the *character*—shifted drastically and drove a change in organizational structure, training, and leadership development. The nations that capitalized on these changes created the greatest advantages in battle.

Almost all developed nations had access to these technologies—Great Britain, France, Germany, the Soviet Union, Japan, and the United States—but it was only the German Wehrmacht that initially optimized all three technological advancements, combining them into a way of war called Blitzkrieg that allowed them to overrun Europe in just 18 months. Germany eventually lost to the overwhelming industrial might of the United States, in conjunction with the Soviet Union and other Allies, but we may not get 18 months to react to a future enemy onslaught.

The impact of the tank

Tanks have been a crucial part of modern warfare for over a century. They are heavily armoured and armed vehicles that provide mobility and firepower on the battlefield . Tanks are used to support ground troops, provide cover and protection, and engage enemy forces from a distance. They are primarily used for offensive operations, spearheading armoured assaults and breakthroughs. Tanks possess the firepower to neutralize enemy fortifications, destroy armoured vehicles, and suppress enemy infantry.

However, tanks are also very costly machines in many aspects. They take a lot of resources to deploy, operate, and procure due to their heavy armour and weight. As a result, in the past thirty years, many concepts have been put forth as tank replacements or supplements in the form of a versatile gun on a lighter wheeled or tracked chassis.

The British Mark 1 tanks could break through defensive lines and rapidly advance into enemy territory, changing the dynamics of warfare. Tanks were able to traverse difficult terrain and withstand enemy fire, providing protection to infantry. They were equipped with machine guns and artillery pieces, which provided important firepower to the infantry. Tanks inspired terror in the enemy and rolled over barbed wire.

Although tanks were slow and easily knocked out by artillery fire, they helped turn the tide on the Western Front. The introduction of tanks revolutionized modern warfare and changed the way battles were fought.

The Mark I tank was a revolutionary invention that forever altered the dynamics of warfare. It was introduced in the Battle of the Somme in 1916 under the command of British General Douglas Haig. The Mark I tank was the first successful tank prototype, known as 'Mother', which completed secret trials in early 1916. The Mark I tank was a symbol of radical change, a testament to human ingenuity in the face of adversity. It was designed to navigate the rutted landscapes and trench networks that characterized the Western Front. Prior to its invention, these trenches, a grim hallmark of World War I, had stymied the armies of both sides, leading to a devastating stalemate.

The Mark I tank's combination of armoured protection, firepower, and all-terrain mobility gave birth to a new era of mechanized warfare, freeing soldiers from the deadly entrapment of trench warfare. The tank, with its caterpillar track design, could navigate the treacherous terrain of the battlefields, clearing paths over trenches and through barbed wire defences . This ability, coupled with its heavy armour and artillery, made it an intimidating force against the German lines.

The Mark I tank had the element of surprise on its side. Its debut on the battlefield at the Battle of Flers-Courcelette caught the Germans off guard, leaving them ill-prepared to counter this new form of warfare. The tank's psychological impact was as significant as its physical one, shaking the resolve of the German forces and signalling the beginning of a shift in the momentum of the war.

The significance of the Mark I tank cannot be overstated. It laid the groundwork for successive generations of tanks, starting from the Mark II to the Mark VIII and beyond. It influenced the design of the German WW1 tank and was a precursor to the formidable tanks of World War II (slightly edited, based upon the Wikipedia explanation).

This study looks to substantiate my thesis that postage stamps can be used to illustrate (almost) any story. The history of the tank is well told on stamps. The tank as a symbol associated with a country's leader is a common theme. The tank is hardly an attractive piece of equipment, but it is used to place events in context of time and event.

Due to the war with China, Japan produced a large number of tanks. Although initially the Japanese used tanks to good effect in their campaigns, full-scale armoured warfare did not occur in the Pacific and Southeast Asian theatres during World War II as it did in Europe, and tank development was neglected in favour of naval activities. Later, during the last year of World War II the newest and best Japanese designs were not used in combat; they were kept back in expectation of defending the Japanese Home Islands.

Tank recognition

Definitely not an expert I have been blessed when the designer incorporates the name of the tank included in the stamp Image. I have included the name if that is the case or if I am sure that my guess is the correct one.

Looking at this study overall it will feature the postage stamp images of some 84 different postal authorities.

The postal authorities included are geographically located :

Europe 14
North America 6
South America 3
Africa 30
Asia 18
Oceania 13

What looks like an anomaly is the number of African countries There are 84 countries in Africa and many of these use Postal Agents to administer their postal system. These agents issue beyond the needs or capabilities of the countries to whom they provide a service but they are a valuable potential revenue source. Selling postage stamps to collectors is a legitimate business. The products, also sold as souvenirs are colourful and attractive. I have also noted the attitude of the Universal Postal Union to such issues. My attitude is that all stamp issues have been designed to tell a story from history – the world's changing history.

The tank was first introduced by Great Britain on the Western Front in Europe during the First World War which had become bogged down in a stalemate based upon trench warfare. The tank potentially afforded a way out of the stalemate.

The 650 or so tank images recognise the tank in different conflicts. These include

World War I	- 54 images
World War II in general	- 341 images
World War II :	
D-Day and The Battle for France	- 63 images
The Battle of Kursk	- 59 images
The Battle of Moscow	- 29 images
The Battle of the Bulge	- 23 Images
The Battle of Stalingrad	- 8 images
The Battle of Berlin	- 5 images
Other battles [i]	- 52 images

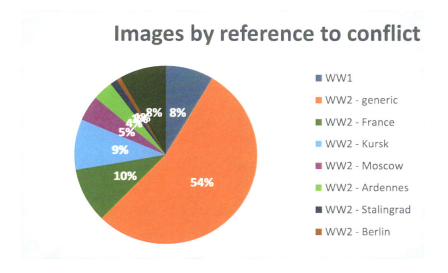

Images by reference to conflict

- WW1
- WW2 - generic
- WW2 - France
- WW2 - Kursk
- WW2 - Moscow
- WW2 - Ardennes
- WW2 - Stalingrad
- WW2 - Berlin

Tanks on postage stamps

In the pages that follow I have reproduced a country's postal authorities in alphabetical order, or their agent's images that place the tank in time and event.

Afghanistan

Afghanistan, officially the Islamic Emirate of Afghanistan, is a landlocked country located at the crossroads of Central Asia and South Asia. Referred to as the Heart of Asia, it is bordered by Pakistan to the east and south, Iran to the west, Turkmenistan to the northwest, Uzbekistan to the north, Tajikistan to the northeast, and China to the northeast and east.

Afghanistan 1979 : Two images, from different issues entitled "The 1st Anniversary of the Communist Takeover".

Afghanistan 1983 : "The 5th Anniversary of the Communist Takeover".

Afghanistan 1985 : One stamp of three representing the 40th anniversary of the end of WW2.

Afghanistan 1988 : "The 10th Anniversary of the Communist Takeover".

The Mujahideen fought against the Soviets in the Soviet–Afghan
War and continued fighting amongst themselves following the Soviets' withdrawal in
1989. The Islamic fundamentalist Taliban controlled most of the country by 1996,
but their Islamic Emirate of Afghanistan received little international recognition
before its overthrow in the 2001 US invasion of Afghanistan. The Taliban returned to
power in 2021 after capturing Kabul and overthrowing the government of
the Islamic Republic of Afghanistan, ending the 2001–2021 war.

Albania

Albania, on Southeastern Europe's Balkan Peninsula, is a small country with
Adriatic and Ionian coastlines and an interior crossed by the Albanian Alps.

Albania 1948 : The 5th Anniversary of the Albanian People's Army. One of a set
of three images.

Alderney

Alderney 2019 : World War II - The 75th Anniversary of D-Day. One of a set of six
images.

Algeria

Algeria is a North African country with a Mediterranean coastline and a Saharan
desert interior.

Algeria 1948 : French stamp overprinted as "General LeClerc Memorial".

Tanks on stamps

Antigua and Barbuda

Antigua and Barbuda is an independent Commonwealth country comprising its 2 namesake islands and several smaller ones. Positioned where the Atlantic and Caribbean meet.

Antigua and Barbuda 1991: The three low value images from a set of nine entitled *World War II*.   The three images are described as (1) US troops cross into Germany, (2) All Axis Forces surrender in North Africa (3) indeterminate.

Australia

Australia 1992 : Australian Troops in World War II. The high value stamp from a set of 5, entitled the Battle of El Alamein.

Azerbaijan

Azerbaijan, the nation and former Soviet republic, is bounded by the Caspian Sea and Caucasus Mountains, which span Asia and Europe.

Azerbaijan 2005 : The 60th Anniversary of the End of World War II.

Counties of issue – in alphabetical order

Belarus

Belarus, officially the Republic of Belarus, is a landlocked country in Eastern Europe. It is bordered by Russia to the east and northeast, Ukraine to the south, Poland to the west, and Lithuania and Latvia to the north-east.

Belarus 1994 : The 50th Anniversary of Liberation of Russia, Belarus and Ukraine .

Belarus 2014 : The 70th Anniversary of the Liberation of Russia, Belarus and Ukraine. The same image is used by Russia but not Ukraine.

Tanks on stamps

Belarus 2019 : The 75th Anniversary of the End of World War II - Liberation of Belarus.

Belarus 2019 : The 75th Anniversary of the End of World War II - Joint Issue with Russia.

A bit of a diversion / following the Russia lead :

Belarus 2021 : The 125th Anniversary of the Birth of Georgy Konstantinovic Zhukov, 1896-1974.

Counties of issue – in alphabetical order

Belgium

Belgium 1950 : One of a set of three 'Charity' stamps, implying support for the fighting soldiers.

Belgium 1957 : Three images from the issue 'In memorial of General Patton'.

Belgium 1965 : One stamp from a four image set 'The 20th anniversary of the end of the Occupation'.

Belgium 1985 : Battle of the Ardennes / The 40th Anniversary of the Liberation, one of a set of three.

Belgium 2004 : The 60th Anniversary of the Battle of the Bulge, one of a set of three.

Belgium 2014 : One of the set of five miniature sheets commemorating the First World War. Bottom right image shows an armoured car – a predecessor of the tank.

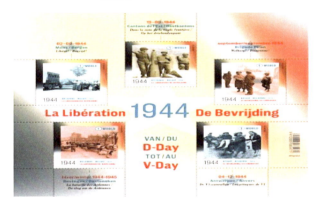

Belgium 2019 : World War II - The 75th Anniversary of the Liberation of Belgium. A Tank is shown in the background of the image in Position (3).

Benin

Benin, officially the Republic of Benin formerly Dahomey, is a country in West Africa. It is bordered by Togo to the west, Nigeria to the east, Burkina Faso to the north-west, and Niger to the north-east. It is a small, tropical country. It is one of the least developed, with an economy heavily dependent on agriculture, and is an exporter of palm oil and cotton. Some employment and income arise from subsistence farming.

Counties of issue – in alphabetical order

Benin 2013 : The 70th anniversary of the Battle of Kursk.

British Indian Ocean Territory

The British Indian Ocean Territory (BIOT), formally known as the Seychelles consist of an archipelago of 58 islands covering some 640,000 sq km of ocean. It is a British Overseas Territory. It is administered from London and is located approximately halfway between East Africa and Indonesia.

British Indian Ocean Territory 1995 : The 50th anniversary of the end of WW2 – Ships and personalities Two images from a set of ten. Five images are of ships. In addition to General Montgomery and General Patton – and their direct involvement in tank warfare the other personalities are General MacArthur, Winston Churchill and Franklin Roosevelt. Several British Commonwealth countries have issued similar sets – of mixed interests when commemorating WW2.

Canada

Canada 1942-1943 : The *Ram Tank*, was a cruiser tank designed and built by Canada in the Second World War, based on the U.S. M3 Medium tank chassis. Two stamps from a definitive issue of sixteen service values.

Tanks on stamps

Canada 1994 and 1995 : The 50th Anniversary of Second World War.

During 1990 to 1995 Canada issues six blocks of four images. Two images look at the use of tanks. 1944 (1) is entitled Walcheren and Scheldt : the Battle of Walcheren Causeway was an engagement of the Battle of the Scheldt between the 5th Canadian Infantry Brigade, elements of the British 52nd Infantry Division and troops of the German 15th Army in 1944. It was the first of many conflicts on and around Walcheren Island during the Scheldt battles. 1945 (3) highlights the liberation of civilians during 1945.

The Central African Republic (formerly known as French Equatorial Africa)

The Central African Republic is a landlocked country in Central Africa. It is bordered by Chad to the north, Sudan to the northeast, South Sudan to the east, the Democratic Republic of the Congo to the south, the Republic of the Congo to the southwest, and Cameroon to the west.

Central African Republic 1994; The 50th anniversary of Allied landings in Normandy. One of two strips each of three images.

Central African Republic 2014 : World War II - The 75th Anniversary of Germany´s Invasion of Poland. The first of two miniature sheets. Number two sheet shows aircrafts.

Central African Republic 2014 : World War II - The 70th Anniversary of the Battle of the Bulge.

Tanks on stamps

Central African Republic 2015 : The 70th Anniversary of the End of World War II.
The middle image of sheet one represents the 1943 Battle of Kursk.

Central African Republic World War II - The 75th Anniversary of the Battle of
Moscow.

The Battle of Moscow was a military campaign that consisted of two periods of
strategically significant fighting on a 600 km (370 mi) sector of the Eastern
Front during World War II, between September 1941 and January 1942. The
Soviet defensive effort frustrated Hitler's attack on Moscow, the capital and
largest city of the Soviet Union. Moscow was one of the primary military and
political objectives for Axis forces in their invasion of the Soviet Union.

The Russian generals acknowledged are (1) Leonid Govorov, (2) Konstantine
Rokossovsky, (3) Lev Dovator, (4) Andrey Neryovsky and (5) Georgy Khukov. The
tank shown in the second sheet is the Russian *Kliment Voroshilov (KV1) Soviet
heavy tank.*

Central African Republic 2017 : The 75th anniversary of the Battle of Stalingrad. Tanks included in sheet One (3) and the background for the second sheet. The personalities featured are Friedrich Paulus and Georgy Zhukov.

Central African Republic 2018 : 100th anniversary of the end of WW1. Three tanks are featured within the first miniature sheet. They show a *Schneider CA1 tank*, a *Mark V tank* and an *Administrative vehicle*. A 2nd miniature sheet features a Bristol 2 aircraft and a newspaper heading.

Tanks on stamps

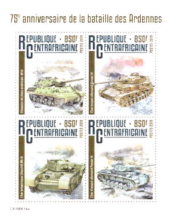

Central African Republic 2019 : The 75th Anniversary of the Battle of Bulge. The military hardware shown within the first sheet are (1) *The US tank destroyer M10*, (2) The *German Medium Tank Panzer IV*, (3) a *Churchill Mk. III* and (4) an earlier *Panzer III*. The background in the higher value service fee issue is a *Churchill Mk. III* and the stamp image a US *M4 Sherman*.

Central African Republic 2019 : World War One (tanks). The military hardware shown within the first sheet are (1*) British Mk. IV*, (2) *French Renault FT 17*, (3) *French Schneider CA1* and finally a *French FCM Heavy tank*. The background in the higher service value is again the *Schneider CA1* and the stamp image is a *German Sturmpanzerwagen A7V, a heavy tank.*

Central African Republic 2019 : World War II - The 75th Anniversary of
Normandy Landings.

The armoured vehicles are, within sheet one (4) a *M8 Greyhound* and the stamp
in the second sheet shows a *Daimler Dingo*.

Central African Republic 2020 : The 80th Anniversary of the Battle of France.
The named tanks are (2) a *German Panzerkampfwagen I*, (3)a *Renault FT* and (4)
a *Matilda Mk. II*. Within the higher value service fee sheet are a *Renault FT* and a
Panzerkampfwagen IV.

Tanks on stamps

CA200505a

Central African Republic 2020 : The 75th Anniversary of the Official End of World War II.

The six events and the relevant tank images are (1) Battle of Stalingrad / *Russian T-34 Tank*, (2) D-Day, (3) Battle of Kursk / *Panzerkampfwagen III*, (4) Battle of Berlin, (5) Battle of the Ardennes / *Cromwell II tank* and (6) the Japanese surrender.

Chad

Chad, officially the Republic of Chad, is an independent state at the crossroads of North and Central Africa. The landlocked country is bordered by Libya to the north, Sudan to the east, the Central African Republic to the south, Cameroon to the southwest, Nigeria to the southwest (at Lake Chad), and Niger to the west.

Chad is another country from which I have had difficulty in accessing on-line records of stamp images for specific years. I suspect that the postal agent supporting the country has a conflict with the catalogue compilers. I have included available images trawled from Ebay sales lists.

Chad 2013 : The Battle of Kursk, 70th anniversary.

The three commanders in the lower value service fee montage are :

(1) Walter Model, German field marshal during World War II. Although he was a hard-driving, aggressive panzer commander early in the war, Model became best known as a practitioner of defensive warfare. His relative success as commander of the Ninth Army in the retreats of 1941–1942 determined his future career path. He has been called the Third Reich's best defensive tactical commander.

(2) Hermann Hoth was a German army commander and war criminal during World War II. He fought in the Battle of France and as a panzer commander on the Eastern Front. Hoth commanded the 3rd Panzer Group during Operation Barbarossa in 1941, and the 4th Panzer Army during the Wehrmacht's 1942 summer offensive.

(3) Hans von Kluge, German field marshal during World War II who held commands on both the Eastern and Western Fronts. He commanded the 4th Army of the Wehrmacht during the invasion of Poland in 1939 and the Battle of France in 1940, earning a promotion to Generalfeldmarschall. Kluge went on to command the 4th Army in Operation Barbarossa and the Battle for Moscow in 1941.

Eric von Manstein and Georgi Joubou are shown within the stamp of the second sheet.

Tanks on stamps

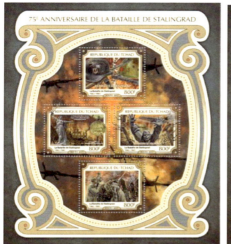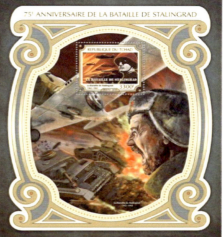

Chad 2017 : World War II - The 75th Anniversary of the Battle of Stalingrad.

Chad 2020 : The End of the First World War.

The two tanks are the Mark IV and the Renault FT - French light tank that was among the most revolutionary and influential tank designs in history. The FT was the first production tank to have its armament within a fully rotating turret.

Counties of issue – in alphabetical order

Czechoslovakia

 Czechoslovakia 1967 : Army Day.

Djibouti

Djibouti is a unitary presidential republic, with executive power resting in the presidency, which is by turn dominant over the cabinet, and legislative power in both the government and the National Assembly. In the early 1990s, tensions over government representation led to armed conflict between Djibouti's ruling People's Rally for Progress (PRP) party and the Front for the Restoration of Unity and Democracy (FRUD) opposition group. The impasse ended in a power-sharing agreement in 2000.

In April 2021, Ismael Guelleh, the second President of Djibouti since independence from France in 1977, was re-elected for his fifth term. Djoubuti has been a prolific issuer of postage stamps, (through its appointed Postal Administration Agent). The *Stampworld* catalogue records stamp issues from 1977 to 2021. A search of Ebay suggests the country has stopped issuing stamps from this date.

Djibouti 2013 : The 70th anniversary of the Battle of Kursk.
Two miniature sheets, 10 stamps. These images show the imperforate sheets.

Tanks on stamps

Djibouti 2018 : A miniature sheet (one of two) commemorating the 100th anniversary of the end of WW1.

Shown is a *Renault FT17 tank* , the portrait is of Marshall Foch.

Djibouti 2020 : The 75th anniversary of the Battle of Iwo Jima.

Tanks shown twice in the lower service fee sheet; position 1 is an *LVT(A)-1* and in position 4 the image is of a *MA2 Sherman*. The vehicle in the second sheet stamp is a jeep but the designer has put an isolated tank into the lower-left corner.

Djibouti 2020 : The 80th Anniversary of the Battle of France. On the low service fee sheet the images are of (i) *German 5dKfz 231* (2) *German Panzer IV* (3) the *Type T13 tank* and in position (4) a *Somlia 5-35 battle tank*. Within the second sheet the vehicles are again a *Panzer IV* and the *Somlia 5-35.*

Djibouti 2020 : Special transport. The modified support vehicle described as a GTK based SplanXtx.

One miniature sheet of two.

Tanks on stamps

Djibouti 2021 : The 80th anniversary of Barbarossa. Two miniature sheets featuring a *Soviet T-26 tank* juxta positioned against the *German Panzer IV*. The second sheet features a Russian *Kilment Voroshlov KV-1.*

Fiji

Fiji 2005 : The 60th Anniversary of the end of World War II. One stamp from the issue of ten Images.

The description within the stamp is *"German King Tiger* in the Ardennes December 1944".

France

 France 1964 : The 20th Anniversary of the Liberation.

France 1969 : The 25th Anniversary of the Battle of the Garigliano.

The Battle of Monte Cassino, also known as the Battle for Rome, was a series of four military assaults by the Allies against German forces in Italy during the Italian Campaign of World War II. The objective was to break through the Winter Line and facilitate an advance towards Rome.
Repeated artillery attacks on assaulting allied troops caused their leaders to incorrectly conclude that the abbey was being used by the Germans as an observation post.

France 1969 : The 25th Anniversary of the Resistance and Liberation. The French leader recognised on the stamp is Maréchal Le Clerk.

France 1969 : The 25th Anniversary of the Liberation of Strassbourg.

France 1994 : The 50th Anniversary of the Liberation of France.

The French Colonies 1940's

In World War II, Charles de Gaulle and the Free French took control of the overseas colonies one-by-one and used them as bases from which they prepared to liberate France. Historian Tony Chafer argues: "In an effort to restore its world-power status after the humiliation of defeat and occupation, France was eager to maintain its overseas empire at the end of the Second World War." However, after 1945 anti-colonial movements began to challenge European authority. Major revolts in Indochina and Algeria proved very expensive and France lost both colonies. After these conflicts, a relatively peaceful decolonization took place elsewhere after 1960.

Tanks on stamps

The concept of a common themed commercial postage stamps for the French Colonies was implemented. The concept was revived by the Free French forces during World War II, who printed eight types of semi-postal stamps in 1943 and 1944. After the Free French landed in Corsica and Southern France, the stamps were used in those areas, and became valid throughout France in November 1944.

Tanks feature in the victory stamps of the colonies. Rather than show the images of every colony I shall select a few, comparisons of colour make them interesting.

The colonies involved include :

Cameroons	Indo-China (Vietnam)
Central African Republic	Madagascar
Comoros	Martenique
French Guyane	New Caledonia
French India	Reunion
French Oceania	St Pierra and Miquela
Guadeloupe	Wallace and Fortuna

Examples of the "1946 The 1st Anniversary of the Victorious End of the Second World War" issue :

Counties of issue – in alphabetical order

Reunion 1946 : Victory issue "From Chad to the Rhine". As well as two other colonies below.The tank battles commemorated : (3) Mareth, (4) Normandie, (5) Paris and (6) Strasbourg.

French India.

Tanks on stamps

Cameroon.

France and French Colonies 1954 : The 10th anniversary of Liberation – logically
Victory issues.
(2). French India, (3) French Oceania and (4) Comoros.

Gabon

Gabon, officially the Gabonese Republic, is a country on the Atlantic coast
of Central Africa, on the equator, bordered by Equatorial Guinea to the
northwest, Cameroon to the north, the Republic of the Congo on the east and
south, and the Gulf of Guinea to the west.

Gabon 1996 : The 50th Anniversary of World War II.

Gabon 1996 : The 50th Anniversary of World War II.

The third in the set of three miniature sheets. Not a tank in sight but the three main players in the Yalta Conference will have known of the value of the tank in battle. Interesting postal history in Gabon. It did not issue stamps during 1939-1959 and it appears not to have issue stamps since 2000.

Tanks on stamps

Gambia

The Gambia, officially the Republic of The Gambia, is a country in West Africa. Geographically, Gambia is the smallest country in continental Africa; it is surrounded by Senegal, except for its western coast on the Atlantic Ocean.

Gambia 2019 : World War II - The 75th Anniversary of D-Day.

Ghana

Ghana, officially the Republic of Ghana, is a country in West Africa. It abuts the Gulf of Guinea and the Atlantic Ocean to the south, sharing borders with Ivory Coast in the west, Burkina Faso in the north, and Togo in the east.

Ghana 1995: The 50th Anniversary of End of Second World War in Europe.

From the previous page I I regard the Ghana commemoration is as a typical "British Commonwealth '50th anniversary year offering. The personalities from top left are : Churchill, Eisenhower, Air Marshall Lord Tedder, Montgomery, General Omar Bradley and De Gaulle. The final image backgrounds tank activity to remember General Patton.

Gibraltar

Gibraltar 2000 : Gibraltar Millenium miniature sheet – bottom row of four stamps out of 16.

Gibraltar 2004 : The 60th Anniversary of D-Day.

Gibraltar 2015 : One stamp from the set of six "The 100th Anniversary of WW1". A *Mk. I tank*.

Tanks on stamps

Great Britain

Great Britain 1994 : The 50th anniversary of D-Day. (5)
The image shows a tank and infantry advancing, Ouistreham. On 6 June 1944, No. 4 Commando landed at Ouistreham (codenamed Sword) and fought their way to Pegasus Bridge, with the 177 Free French of the No. 10 (Inter-Allied) Commando given the honour of spearheading the advance. The assault on Ouistreham was featured in the movie *The Longest Day*.

Great Britain 2019 : The 75th anniversary of D-Day. (3) Sows the 50th Division landing on Gold Beach.

Great Britain 2021 : British Army vehicles. Eight vehicles are shown.

As shown on the previous page the vehicle descriptions are :

The Mark IV was a British tank of the First World War. Introduced in 1917.

(1) The Infantry Tank Mark II, best known as *the Matilda*, is a British infantry tank of the Second World War. It was the only British tank to serve from the start of the war to its end.

(2) Officially designated as 'Tank, Infantry, Mk.IV, A.22', *the Churchill* entered service with the British Armoured Forces in 1941.

(3) *The Centurion* was the primary British Army main battle tank of the post-World War II period. Introduced in 1945, it is widely considered to be one of the most successful post-war tank designs, remaining in production into the 1960s, and seeing combat into the 1980s.

(4) *The FV101 Scorpion* is a British armoured reconnaissance vehicle, and also a light tank. It was the lead vehicle and the fire support type in the Combat Vehicle Reconnaissance (Tracked), CVR(T), family of seven armoured vehicles.

(5) *The FV4201 Chieftain* was the main battle tank (MBT) of the United Kingdom from the 1960s into 1990s.

(6) *The FV4034 Challenger 2* (MoD designation "CR2") is a third generation British main battle tank (MBT) in service with the armies of the United Kingdom, Oman, and Ukraine.

(7) *The Ajax*, formerly known as the Scout SV (Specialist Vehicle), is a group of armoured fighting vehicles being developed by General Dynamics UK for the British Army.

A second miniature sheet was issued in conjunction to the British Army Vehicles shown above. They do not conform to the definition of a tank. But for completeness they are listed here : (1) *Coyote tactical support vehicle*, (2) *Army Wildcat helicopter*, (3) *Trojan Armoured vehicle of the Royal Engineers* and (4) the *Foxhound Light protected patrol vehicle*.

Grenada

Grenada is a Caribbean country comprising a main island, also called Grenada, and smaller surrounding islands.

Set continued on the next page ....

Tanks on stamps

Grenada 1970 : The 25th Anniversary of Ending of World War II.
Tanks feature (2) The Fall of Berlin and Marshal Zhukov and (6) the Battle of El Alamein and General Montgomery.

Grenada 1990 : The 50th Anniversary of Second World War.
Four images from a mixed image issue of ten. From left to right the images represent (1). British tanks during Operation Battleaxe, 1941, (2) Allied tank in Southern France, 1944, (3) Hoisting the US flag on Leyte, Philippines, 1944 and (4) US tanks entering Cologne, 1945.

Grenada 1974 : The 100th Anniversary of the Birth of Sir Winston Churchill, 1874-1965

Grenada 1994 : The 50th anniversary of D-Day. Multiple roles for the tank.[2]

Grenada 2005 : "Remembering VE Day".

---

[2] I am reminded by Quora (15.v.24) of the British soldiers' ability to improvise and innovate. One example of this is the creation of the "Hobart's Funnies." These were specialized tanks developed by Major General Percy Hobart to overcome the unique challenges posed during the Normandy landings. From tanks equipped with flamethrowers to devices that could lay bridges across obstacles, these ingenious contraptions played a crucial role in the success of the D-Day invasion. See also the miniature sheet on the next page from the Grenada Grenadines.

Grenada Grenadines

The Grenadines are a group of 35 small islands located between Grenada and St. Vincent in the Windward Islands of the Lesser Antilles. A separate postal authority to Grenada.

Grenada Grenadines 1990 : The 50th Anniversary of Second World War. 5 tank images from within the set of ten. The designer has included a description of each image but these are not legible. The only image I am confident of naming is the $1 image representing the Battle of the Bulge; an *M40 Sherman*.

Grenada Grenadines 1994 : The 50th anniversary of D-Day. Multiple roles for the tank. This set of four images is very similar to that issued by Grenadines. The three low service fee stamps are similar images but the miniature sheet shows the tank in a different role.

Guinea

Guinea officially the Republic of Guinea is a coastal country in West Africa. It borders the Atlantic Ocean to the west, Guinea-Bissau to the northwest, Senegal to the north, Mali to the northeast, Cote d'Ivoire to the southeast, and Sierra Leone and Liberia to the south.[3]

Guinea 1991 : Battles of the Second World War.

Two images from the set of six. 1. The Battle of El Alamein / Generals Rommel and Montgomery 1942. 2. The Battle of the Ardennes 1944. Generals Guderian and Patton. A miniature sheet completed the issue with a portrait of Dwight Eisenhower.

Guinea -Bissau

Guinea-Bissau , officially the Republic of Guinea-Bissau is a country in West Africa. The country has been a prolific issuer of postage stamps, (through its appointed Postal Administration Agent). The *Stampworld* catalogue records stamp issues from 1974 to 2018. A search of Ebay suggests the country has stopped issuing stamps.

---

[3] The catalogue I generally use is Stampworld. But it is not as complete as it claims to be. Guinea is one country that Stampworld seems to have abandoned It shows no year issues beyond 2013. Issues from later years do occasionally appear on Ebay. I have included what I can find, after a diligent search but I know I do not have every stamp there will be.

Tanks on stamps

Guinea-Bissau 2014 : The 100th Anniversary of the beginning of World War I. This is the second of a two-sheet issue – showing the potential of armoured vehicles. The two featured leaders are Archduke Franz Ferdinand of Austria and King Joseph of Austria.

Guinea-Bissau 2014 : The 75th Anniversary of the German Invasion of Poland. Two Miniature sheets.

The portraits of Churchill and de Gaulle are clear on the previous page as is
Heinz Guderian on the second sheet. Previously unknown to me is the other
portrait. He is Marshal Edward Rydz-Śmigły, also called Edward Śmigły-Rydz, a
Polish politician, statesman, Marshal of Poland and Commander-in-Chief of
Poland's armed forces, as well as a painter and poet. The armoured vehicles are
anonymous.Heinz Wilhelm Guderian was a German general during World War II.
He was an early pioneer and advocate of the "blitzkrieg" approach, he played a
central role in the development of the panzer division concept. In 1936, he
became the Inspector of Motorized Troops.

Guinea-Bissau 2014 : The 70th Anniversary of the Liberation of Paris.
Two miniature sheets.

Guinea Bissau 2015 : World War II - The 70th Anniversary of the Death of Anne
Frank, 1929-1945.
Image (3) marks the Battle of Stalingrad and (4) The Battle of Kursk.

Tanks on stamps

Guinea-Bissau 2018 : The 100th Anniversary of the End of World War I.
In both sheets the tank is designated as a *Mark V.*

BATALHA DE KURSK

BATALHA DE KURSK

Guinea-Bissau 2018 : The Battle of Kursk.
On the first sheet the tanks are; Position (4) *KV1 Panzerjager Tiger* (5) *Tiger 1* (6)
Su-152 Panther. On the high value sheet are the *T 34 tank* and the *Tiger 1*.

Guyana

Guyana, officially the Co-operative Republic of Guyana, is a country on the northern coast of South America, part of the historic mainland British West Indies.

Guyana 1993 : The 50th Anniversary of Second World War.
Two stamps from a set of ten. Both tank images purport to show 1944 US tank activity in France. In addition, Guyana issued a miniature sheet as part of the issue portraying American and Russian troops meeting at the Elbe River.

Guyana 1994 : The 50th Anniversary of Second World War – D-Day Mulberry Harbour.
A ten-stamp miniature sheet telling the D-Day story with tanks contributing, once landed in France.

Guyana 2004 : The 60th Anniversary Tribute to the D-Day Landings.
Two of seven miniature sheets commemorating both events and personalities.
The designer has included the names and affiliations of the soldiers he recognises.

Michael Wittmann, 101st Sturmmorser Kompanie,

Lieutenant Robert Edlin, 2nd Battalion Army Ranger,

CSM Stanley Hollis, 6th Green Howards, and

Kurt Meyer, 12th SS Panzer Division.

Hardly a role model, I note part of the Wikipedia description of Kurt Meyer;
Kurt Meyer (1910 – 1961) was an SS commander and convicted war
criminal of Nazi Germany. He served in the Waffen-SS (the combat branch of the
SS) and participated in the Battle of France, Operation Barbarossa, and other
engagements during World War II. Meyer commanded the 12th SS Panzer
Division Hitlerjugend during the Allied invasion of Normandy, and was a
recipient of the Knight's Cross of the Iron Cross with Oak Leaves and Swords.
After ordering the mass murder of civilians and prisoners of war (POWs) several
times during the conflict, Meyer was convicted of war crimes for his role in
the Ardenne Abbey massacre (the murder of Canadian POWs in Normandy). He
was sentenced to death, but the sentence was later commuted to life in prison.

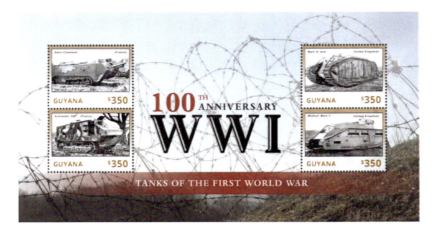

Guyana 2014 : Tanks of the First World War.

Images show two French models; a *Saint-Chamond* and a *Schneider C41F.* The two British models are the *Mark IV* and a *Medium Marc C.* The Medium Mark C Hornet was a British tank developed during the First World War, but produced too late to see any fighting.

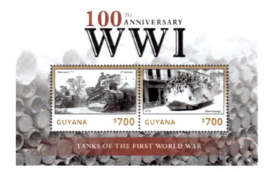

Guyana 2014 : The 2nd miniature sheet shows images of a *French Renaud FT* and a *German A7V.*

Guyana 2017 : American war posters. "World War II 75th Anniversary.

Guyana 2020 Vietnam War - Tet Offensive - The Battle of the Hue.

The Battle of Huế in 1968, also called the siege of Huế, was a major military engagement in the Tết Offensive launched by North Vietnam and the Việt Cộng during the Vietnam War. After initially losing control of most of Huế and its surroundings, the combined South Vietnamese and American forces gradually recaptured the city over one month of intense fighting. The battle was one of the longest and bloodiest of the war, and the battle negatively affected American public perception of the war.

Counties of issue – in alphabetical order

Hungary

Hungary 1941 : Soldiers' Gift Foundation – one image from set of five.

Hungary 1951 : 1951-1953 "Five Years' Plan. One of 14 service values.

Hungary 1951 : National Army Day.

India

India 1989 : The 3rd Cavalry Regiment.

Also known as the Brave Rifles, the III Armored Corps' Cavalry Regiment, capable of operating as a Reconnaissance and Security force or close with and destroy as a Stryker Brigade Combat Team.

India : 2002 Indian Ordinance Factories 1802-2002.

Tanks on stamps

India 2006 : The 62 Cavalry.

The 62nd Cavalry is an armoured regiment of the Indian Army and was raised by
Lt Col RS Butalia on 31 Mar 1957 at Ambala cantonment. Drawn from the
existing cavalry regiments of the time, the 62nd Cavalry was recruited
from Sikh, Jat and Dogra communities.

India 2009 : The 2nd Lancers.

The 2nd Lancers (Gardner's Horse) is one of the oldest and a highly decorated
armoured regiment of the Indian Army. The regiment was formed by the
amalgamation of two of the oldest regiments of the Bengal Army – the 2nd
Royal Lancers (Gardner's Horse) and the 4th Cavalry.

India 2023 : The 75th anniversary of the Indian Army.

Iraq

Iraq 1963 : Army Day. (Four from the full set of eight).

(from the previous page)… .Abdul-Karim Qasim Muhammad Bakr al-Fadhli al-Zubaidi (1914 – 1963) was the Iraqi military officer and nationalist who came to power in 1958 when the Iraqi monarchy was overthrown during the 14 July Revolution.

Iraq 2021 : Army Day – the full set of four.

Ivory Coast

Ivory Coast, also known as Côte d'Ivoire and officially the Republic of Côte d'Ivoire, is a country on the southern coast of West Africa. It borders Guinea to the northwest, Liberia to the west, Mali to the northwest, Burkina Faso to the northeast, Ghana to the east, and the Gulf of Guinea (Atlantic Ocean) to the south. With 30.9 million inhabitants in 2023, Ivory Coast is the third-most populous country in West Africa.

Ivory Coast 2013 : The 70th anniversary of the Battle of Kursk.
The two personalities shown within the stamp images are Eric von Manstein and Gueorgiu Joukov with their respective main tanks, the *Panzerkampfwagen V Panther* and the Russian KV-1.

Tanks on stamps

Ivory Coast 2018 : Tanks of the Second World War.

Isle of Man

Isle of Man 2016 : One stamp from the set of six "The 100th Anniversary of WWI
- The Battle of the Somme".

Counties of issue – in alphabetical order

Isle of Man 2016 : One stamp from the set of six "The 300th Anniversary of the Royal Artillery.

Jersey

Jersey 2014 : The D-day landings. (0ne of a set of six images).

Jersey 2016 : The 100th Anniversary of World War I - Battles. Miniature sheet. A Mark 1 tank.

Jordan

Jordan 1965 : Army Day commemoration.

Tanks on stamps

Kazakhstan

Kazakhstan, a Central Asian country and former Soviet republic, extends from the Caspian Sea in the west to the Altai Mountains at its eastern border with China and Russia.

Kazakhstan 1995 : The 50th Anniversary of End of Second World War.

The lady, with the tank in the background, shows Aliya Moldagulova, a Kazakh woman sniper of the Red Army during World War II who killed over 30 Nazi soldiers. After dying of wounds sustained in battle on 14 January 1944, she was posthumously awarded the title Hero of the Soviet Union.

Kiribati

Kiribati, officially the Republic of Kiribati, is an island country in the Micronesia subregion of Oceania in the central Pacific Ocean.

Kiribati 2005 : (2 stamps from the set of 10 images) The 60th Anniversary of the End of World War II - "The Route to Victory".

The two tanks are described on the stamps as a *Japanese Type 95 Ha-Go* and the opposing *M40 Sherman* of C Company on Tarawa Beach, 20.xi.43.

Kuwait

Kuwait is situated in the northern edge of Eastern Arabia at the tip of the Persian Gulf, bordering Iraq to the north and Saudi Arabia to the south. In 1990, after oil production disputes with neighbouring Iraq, Kuwait was invaded, and later annexed into one of Iraq's governorates by Iraq under Saddam Hussein. The Iraqi occupation of Kuwait came to an end on February 26, 1991, after military intervention by a military coalition led by the United States and various other countries.

   Kuwait 1991 : "Liberation".

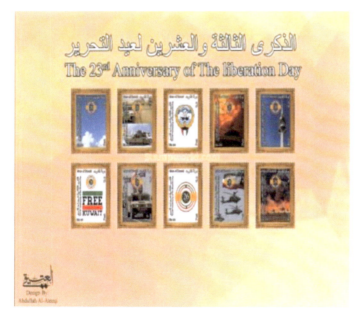 Kuwait 2014 : The 23rd Anniversary of Liberation Day. (Reduced in the scan).

Tanks on stamps

Kyrgyzstan

Kyrgyzstan, officially the Kyrgyz Republic, is a landlocked country in Central Asia, lying in the Tian Shan and Pamir Mountain ranges.

Kyrgyzstan 2010 : The 65th Anniversary of the End of World War II. The same images – a gummed stamp and a self-adhesive alternative.

Laos

Laos, officially the Lao People's Democratic Republic is the only landlocked country in Southeast Asia. At the heart of the Indochinese Peninsula, Laos is bordered by Myanmar and China to the northwest, Vietnam to the east, Cambodia to the southeast, and Thailand to the west and southwest. Its capital and largest city is Vientiane.

Laos 1985 : The 40th Anniversary of End of Second World War. The Battles of Kursk and Berlin; two images from the set of five.

Latvia

Latvia officially the Republic of Latvia , is a country in the Baltic region of Northern Europe. It is one of the three Baltic states, along with Estonia to the north and Lithuania to the south. It borders Russia to the east, Belarus to the southeast, and shares a maritime border with Sweden to the west.

Latvia 2019 : The 100th Anniversary of the Latvian Army.

Liberia

Liberia, officially the Republic of Liberia, is a country on the West African coast. It is bordered by Sierra Leone to its northwest, Guinea to its north, Ivory Coast to its east, and the Atlantic Ocean to its south and southwest.

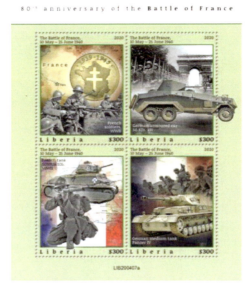

Liberia 2020 : The 80th anniversary of the Battle of France.
The tank images are (3) a Free French cavalry tank a *SOMUA S-35,* (4) the German medium tank – the *Panther IV.*

Libya

With an area of almost 1.8 million km, Libya is the fourth-largest country in Africa and the Arab world, and the 16th-largest in the world.

Libya 1995 : The 9th Anniversary of American Aggression.

Tanks on stamps

Luxembourg

In 1940, Germany occupied the nominally neutral Luxembourg . The Nazis were not prepared to allow Luxembourgers self-government, and gradually integrated Luxembourg into the Third Reich by informally attaching the country administratively to a neighbouring German province. After the war, Luxembourg ended its neutrality and became an integral part of Europe.

Luxembourg 1947 : George Patton.

Madagascar

Madagascar, officially the Republic of Madagascar, is an island country comprising the island of Madagascar and numerous smaller peripheral islands. Lying off the southeastern coast of Africa, it is the world's fourth largest island, the second-largest island country and the 44th largest country in the world.

Madagascar 2013 : The Battle of Kursk, 70th anniversary.

Mali

Mali, officially the Republic of Mali, is a landlocked country in West Africa. Mali is the eighth-largest country in Africa. The country is bordered to the north by Algeria, to the east by Niger, to the northwest by Mauritania, to the south by Burkina Faso and Ivory Coast, and to the west by Guinea and Senegal.

Mali 1994 : The 50th Anniversary of Second World War D-Day Landings. Two of five strips of three stamps. These examples vividly show the land battle component of the assault.

Mali 2015 : The Battle of Kursk; main players.

The featured commanders are :

Nikolai Vatutin (1901–1944) a Soviet military commander during World War II who was responsible for many Red Army operations in the Ukrainian SSR as the commander of the Southwestern Front, and of the Voronezh Front during the Battle of Kursk.

Ivan Konev (1897-1973), a Soviet general and Marshal of the Soviet Union who led Red Army forces on the Eastern Front during World War II, responsible for retaking much of Eastern Europe from occupation by the Axis Powers.

Tanks on stamps

Günther von Kluge, also known as Hans Günther von Kluge (1882-1944), the German field marshal during World War II who held commands on both the Eastern and Western Fronts.
Walter Model (1891-1945), German field marshal during World War II. Although he was a hard-driving, aggressive panzer commander early in the war, Model became best known as a practitioner of defensive warfare.

Maldives

The Maldives is southwest of Sri Lanka and India, about 750 kilometres (470 miles; 400 nautical miles) from the Asian continent's mainland. The Maldives' chain of 26 atolls stretches across the equator from Ihavandhippolhu Atoll in the north to Addu Atoll in the south.

The Maldives has been a prolific issuer of postage stamps, (through its appointed Postal Administration Agent). The *Stampworld* catalogue records stamp issues from 1906 to 2020. A search of Ebay suggests that *Stampworld* may have stopped cataloguing Maldive stamps.

Maldives 2014 : World War II - The 70th Anniversary of the Battle of the Bulge. I cannot recognise the tanks illustrated.

Maldives 2014 : The 100th anniversary of the beginning of WW1. The personalities shown in the first sheet are Willhelm II, the German Emperor and Joseph Joffre, the French general who served as Commander-in-Chief of French forces on the Western Front from the start of World War I until the end of 1916. The tank shown is a *Mark 1*. Within sheet two, Joseph Gallieni is the French general who served as Commander-in-Chief of French forces on the Western Front from the start of World War I until the end of 1916.The tank providing context is a *Renault FT-1762 tank*.

Maldives 2015 : World War II - The 70th Anniversary of the Liberation of Paris. The tank illustrated is the *Renault FT-17.* The Renault FT was a light tank deployed in 1918. Unlike the earlier French tanks it was designed to accompany infantry in large numbers to swamp the enemy like a "swarm of bees" (Gen. Estienne - creator of the French tank force). The Renault FT was sold to many countries after WW1 and was still in service with the French Army at the start of WW2.

Tanks on stamps

Maldives 2015 : The 70th anniversary of the end of WWII.
The use of the tank in an urban confrontation is shown in the first sheet.

Maldives 2016 : World War II - The 75th Anniversary of the Battle of Moscow.

The two featured soldiers within the first sheet are generals Georgy Zhukov and Fedor von Bock. During the Battle of Moscow newly built *T-34 tanks* were concealed in the woods as German armour rolled past them; as a scratch team of Soviet infantry contained their advance, Soviet armour attacked from both flanks and savaged the *German Panzer IV tanks*.

Maldives 2017 World War II - The 75th Anniversary of the Battle of Stalingrad. A wrecked German tank serves as an endorsement.

Maldives 2018 : The 75th Anniversary of the Battle of Kursk.
The tank images used are (1) The *Russian T-34*, (2) *251D half-track*, (3) a *Medium Tank T-34/76*, (4) *German Tiger 1*, and on the second sheet (1) *Russian KV-1 tank* and (background) a *German heavy tank Tiger 1*.

Maldives 2018 : (Modern) Military vehicles.

Tanks on stamps

(Narrative from the previous page) - Sheet 1 position (3) the image is of a M113. Sheet two shows a Leopard 2A7+ with a BPM-97 as the background and context. The Leopard 2 is a third-generation German main battle tank. Developed by Krauss-Maffei in the 1970s, the tank entered service in 1979 and replaced the earlier Leopard 1 as the main battle tank of the West German army. The BPM-97 or Выстрел is the Russian military designation for the KAMAZ 43269 Vystrel 4×4 wheeled mine-resistant; ambush protected vehicle.

Maldives 2019 : The 75th anniversary of the Normandy Landings. Sheet 1, position (4) shows a Sherman Firefly. The Sherman Firefly was a medium tank used by the United Kingdom and some armoured formations of other Allies in the Second World War. It was based on the US M4 Sherman but was fitted with the more powerful British 76.2 mm calibre 17-pounder anti-tank gun as its main weapon.

Maldives 2019 : The 70th anniversary of NATO.

Sheet 1, position (4) shows an M1 Abrams. The M1 Abrams is a third-generation American main battle tank designed by Chrysler Defence and named for General Creighton Abrams.

Maldives 2019 : The 105th Anniversary of the Beginning of WWI.

Sheet 1, position (4) shows a *Mark 1*, also shown as the background for the second sheet.

Maldives 2019 : World War II - The 75th Anniversary of the Battle of the Bulge. Sheet 1, position (1) shows a *US M4*, position (4) *German Panzer V Panther*. Within the second sheet the stamp illustrates a *erman Jagdpanzer 38,* originally the *Leichter Panzerjäger 38(t),* known mostly post-war as *Hetzer*, which was a German light tank destroyer of the Second World War based on a modified Czechoslovakian Panzer 38(t) chassis. and within the snowy background are an *American M4* and a *German Panzer 5 Panther*.

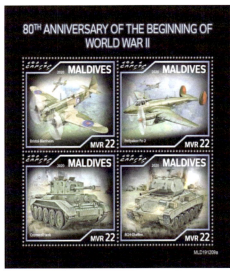

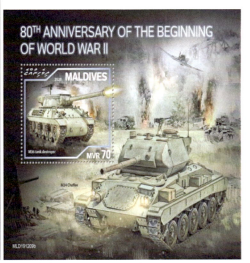

Maldives 2020 : 80th anniversary of the beginning of WW2.

Counties of issue – in alphabetical order

From the previous page - Sheet 1, position (3) shows a Cromwell tank and position (4) is a M24 Chaffee. The sheet two stamp is a M36 tank destroyer and a M24 Chaffee as the background image.

Marshall Islands

The Marshall Islands , officially the Republic of the Marshall Islands is an island country west of the International Date Line and north of the equator in the Micronesia region in the Northwestern Pacific Ocean. The territory consists of 29 coral atolls and five islands divided across two island chains. During the 1990s The Third party philatelic provider, Unicover Corporation of Wyoming, (1990-2017) issued 100 images in a most complete series of stamps entitled "History of the Second World War". Those which show a tank are reproduced below.

Marshall Islands 1990 :   History of the Second World War - Invasions of Denmark and Norway, 1940.

Marshall Islands 1991 : History of the Second World War - Battle of Beda Fomm, 1941.

The Battle of Beda Fomm took place following the rapid British advance during Operation Compass (9 December 1940 – 9 February 1941). The Italian 10th Army was forced to evacuate Cyrenaica, the eastern province of Libya. In late January, the British learned that the Italians were retreating along the Litoranea Balbo from Benghazi. The 7th Armoured Division was dispatched to intercept the remnants of the 10th Army by moving through the desert, south of the Jebel Akhdar (Green Mountain) via Msus and Antelat as the 6th Australian Division pursued the Italians along the coast road, north of the jebel. The terrain was hard going for the British tanks and Combeforce a flying column of wheeled vehicles, was sent ahead across the chord of the jebel.

Marshall Islands 1991 : History of the Second World War - German Invasion of Balkans, 1941.

Marshall Islands 1991 : History of the Second World War - German Invasion of Russia, 1941.

Marshall Islands 1991 : History of the Second World War - Siege of Moscow, 1941.

As an indication of the thoroughness of the Marshall Islands postal administration to record the history of WW2, I note that during 1992, in addition to the Images I am showing here, the following 1942 events were recorded in a similar style; the Arcadia Conference, Washington D.C., the Capture of Rabaul by Japan, the Battle of the Java Sea, the Japanese Landing on New Guinea, the Evacuation of General Douglas MacArthur from Corregidor, the British raid on Saint Nazaire, the Surrender of Bataan, the Doolittle Raid on Tokyo, the Fall of Corregidor to Japan, the Battle of the Coral Sea, the Battle of Midway, the Destruction of Lidice, Czechoslovakian Village, the German Capture of Sevastopol, the Destruction of Convoy PQ-17, the US Marine Landing on Guadalcanal, the Battle of Savo Island, the British Dieppe Raid, the Battle of

Stalingrad, the Battle of Eastern Solomon Islands, the Battle of Cape Esperance, and the Battle of Barents Sea.

Marshall Islands 1992 ; History of the Second World War - Fall of Manila to Japan, 1942.

Marshall Islands 1992 : History of the Second World War - Capture of Rangoon by Japan, 1942.

Marshall Islands 1992 : History of the Second World War - Battle of El Alamein, 1942.

Marshall Islands 1993 : History of the Second World War - Liberation of Kharkov, 1943.

Tanks on stamps

Marshall Islands 1993 : History of the Second World War - Battle of Kursk, 1943.

Marshall Islands 1993 : History of the Second World War - Allied Invasion of Sicily, 1943. Generals George Patton and Bernard Montgomery.

Marshall Islands 1994 : History of the Second World War - Warsaw Uprising, 1944.

Marshall Islands 1994 : The Liberation of Paris 1944.

Marshall Islands 1994 :
Peleliu Battle Tank aka Armoured Amphibious Tractor LVT(A)-4.

Marshall Islands 1944 : The Battle of the Bulge.
The two officers shown (4) are Lieutenant Colonel Creighton Abrams and
Brigadier-General Anthony McAuliffe.

Marshall Islands 1995 : History of the Second World War - U.S.
Capture of Remagen Bridge, Germany, 1945.

Marshall Islands 1995 : History of the Second World War -
Capture of Berlin by Soviet Troops, 1945. Portrait shows Marshal Georgy Khukov.

Marshall Islands 1995 : History of the Second World War
V-J, Victory in Japan Day, 1945. (No tanks but significant).

Tanks on stamps

Mozambique

Moçambique, is a country located in southeast Africa bordered by the Indian Ocean to the east, Tanzania to the north, Malawi and Zambia to the northwest, Zimbabwe to the west, and Eswatini and South Africa to the southwest.

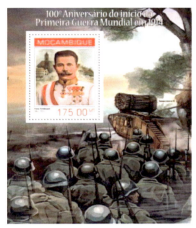

Mozambique 2014 : The 100th Anniversary of the Start of World War I. Archduke Franz Ferdinand is shown within a background of soldiers and a *Mark 4 tank* with a mat laying capacity. The second sheet of a set of two.

Mozambique 2018 : The 100th Anniversary of the End of World War I. The designer recognises the impact of the tank (showing a *Mark V tank*) during a break in the action.

Myanmar

Myanmar, officially the Republic of the Union of Myanmar and also known as Burma (the official name until 1989), is a country in Southeast Asia. It is the largest country by area in Mainland Southeast Asia and has a population of about 55 million. It is bordered by Bangladesh and India to its northwest, China to its northeast, Laos and Thailand to its east and southeast, and the Andaman Sea and the Bay of Bengal to its south and southwest.

Myanmar 2020 : One stamp from the set of three "Armed Forces Day".

Nauru

Nauru, officially the Republic of Nauru and formerly known as Pleasant Island, is an island country and microstate in Micronesia, part of Oceania in the Central Pacific. Its nearest neighbour is Banaba of Kiribati, about 300 km to the east.

Nauru 1995 : The 60th anniversary of the end of World War II.
One image from a set of 10 stamps and a miniature sheet. This image illustrates a *Japanese Type 97 Te-Ka* tank.

New Caledonia

New Caledonia is a French territory comprising dozens of islands in the South Pacific.

New Caledonia 1954 : The 10th Anniversary of Landing of Allied Forces in Normandy. See also the notes upon the French Colonies

Tanks on stamps

New Zealand

New Zealand 1984 : New Zealand Military history.
The *Valentine tank* was used in the later stages of the WW2 battles.

New Zealand 1990 : General Bernard Freyberg, commander of the Allied forces
during the battle for control of Crete in 1941. One of a set of six "Famous New
Zealanders".

New Zealand 2017 : "The darkest hour"
A miniature sheet of six images and the background mention of Passchendaele
Ridge as the main context for the six images. In all 30 images were issued over
the five years' WW1 review. In position (4) the image of a *Mark 1*.

Counties of issue – in alphabetical order

New Zealand 2020 : Peter Weir's WW2 paintings.
(3) the Battle of El Alamein. I reason the tank to be a *Sherman M4*.

Nicaragua

Nicaragua, is the largest country in Central America, bordered by Honduras to the north, the Caribbean to the east, Costa Rica to the south, and the Pacific Ocean to the west.

"OPERACIÓN SUPREMA" DIA "D" 6 DE JUNIO DE 1944

Nicaragua 1994 : The 50th Anniversary of D-Day. (5) image is described as a *Churchill AVRE*.

Niger

Niger, officially the Republic of the Niger, is a landlocked country in West Africa. It is a unitary state bordered by Libya to the northeast, Chad to the east, Nigeria to the south, Benin and Burkina Faso to the southwest, Mali to the west, and Algeria to the northwest.

Niger 2014 : World War I - The 100th Anniversary of the beginning of the First World War in 1914.

The *Renault FT* is by far the most well-known French tank of the First World War, but it was not the first *Char d'Assaut* used by the French Army. In 1917 the Schneider 'C.A.1' and the Saint-Chamond were sent into battle for the first time. The two personalities are General Foch and Archduke Franz Ferdinand of Austria.

Niger 2014 : World War Two.

The personalities featured are William Halsey, Carl Gustaf Mannerheim of Finland and Churchill. The tank is described as a *Russian T-36*.

Niger 2015 : The 70th anniversary of the end of WW2.

The personalities are President Roosevelt, Dwight Eisenhower, Bernard Montgomery (and I guess Dougas MacArthur) and Winston Churchill.

Niger 2015 : The Battle of Moscow.
The personalities are Fedor von Bock and Georgy Khukov. The designer has labelled the tank on the high-value sheet as a *Panzer IV*.

Niger 2017 : The 75th anniversary of the Battle of Stalingrad.
The personalities are Yakov Pavlov and Friedrich Paulus. Shown within both miniature sheet is Vasile Chuikov. The tanks are labelled as *a T-34/76* and a *Panzerkampfwagen III*.

Niger 2017 : The 90th anniversary of the Peoples' Liberation Army. As Far as I can tell the tank in the foreground of the 900F image is the *Chinese Type 99*. It is labelled a *Type 99* on the miniature sheet.

During 2018 Niger also commemorated the 100th anniversary of the end of WW1. No armoured vehicles were used as images – but somehow Prince Willam is portrayed (but not shown here)?

Niger 2018 : The 100th Anniversary of the WW1 Second Battle of Somme. Sheet 1 (1) shows a *British Mark 1.* On the second sheet the designer has drawn the *German* Sturmpanzerwagen *A7V* tank.

Niger 2019 : The 80th Anniversary of the Beginning of World War II.

The vehicles within the first sheet are (1) a *Russian BA-10 armoured car* and (4) *T-18 light tank*, also shown as the background and context for the second sheet.

Niger 2019 : World War II - The 75th Anniversary of the Battle of the Bulge. The vehicles shown in sheet one on the previous page are (1) A *German assault gun Sturmgeschultz III*, (2) *Assault gun Sturmtiger*, (3) A British Cromwell Mk.VIII tank and (4) the US self-propelled M7 Priest. Dwight Eisenhower is shown with a British *Cromwell tank* within the high service value sheet.

Niger 2020 : The 80th Anniversary of the Battle of France. Two different formats with images (1), a French Somus 5-40, (2) a German a *Panzerkampfwagen IV,* and (3) *Char B1 Bis (French)*.

Niger 2021 : The 80th Anniversary of the Operation Barbarossa. The tanks images, above / left show a *Soviet KV-1* at the top and below a *German Panzer III Ausf.H.* The two personalities are Gueorgui Joukov (spelling as used on the stamp) and Erich von Manstein. A *Russian T-34* is shown on the smaller sheet.

Niger 2021 : The 30th Anniversary of the Dissolution of the Soviet Union. Mikhael Gorborchev features, as do the images of tanks, on both sheets.

The 2021 image reused to recognise the Russian Invasion of Ukraine.

Niger 2022 : The 80th anniversary of the end of the Battle of Moscow. The tanks show on sheet one above are (1) *German Panzer 18(t)*, (2) *Soviet T-34*, (3) *Soviet SU-100* and (4) a *Panzer III*. The personalities are Franz Halder, who earlier in the war had directed the planning and implementation of Operation Barbarossa and Gueorgiu Joukov.

Niger 2022 : The 55th anniversary of the Six-Day War.

The tanks shown on the previous page are (2) a *PT-76*, a Soviet amphibious light tank that was introduced in the early 1950s and soon became the standard reconnaissance tank of the Soviet Army and the other Warsaw Pact armed forces.(3) The *AMX-13* is a French light tank produced from 1952 to 1987. It served with the French Army and was exported to more than 26 other countries. On the smaller sheet the stamp image is of a *Panzer 2*. The larger background image illustrates an US *M-51 Super Sherman*.

Niger 2022 : The 80th Anniversary of the First Battle of El Alamein. Sheet one; (1) The *British infantry Valentine tank*, (3) the vehicle is *a Sd.Kfz. 250 (German: Sonderkraftfahrzeug 250*; 'special motor vehicle'), a light armoured half-track and (4) a Panzer II Ausf C. The soldiers featured are Sir Claude Auckinleck, Edwin Rommel and Estore Bastico.
In addition to the image of a supporting Hawker Hurricane the two tanks on the stamp are a *Valentine* (back) and a *Sherman tank*. In the larger scene the tanks are a *German Panzer III* and an Italian Fiat-Analdo M13/40.

Tanks on stamps

Niger 2020 : The 80th
Anniversary of the Operation
Uranus.
Operation Uranus was the
codename of the Soviet Red
Army's 19–23 November 1942
strategic operation on
the Eastern Front of World War
II which led to
the encirclement of Axis forces in
the vicinity of Stalingrad:
the German Sixth Army, the Third
and Fourth Romanian armies,
and portions of the
German Fourth Panzer Army.
The tanks on show are (1) *a*
Sturmescholtz III, (2) A *Soviet BA-*
64 and (4) A *Soviet T-70*. The
competing generals portrayed in
sheet two are Friedrich Paulus
and Gueorgiu Joukov.

The third sheet in the set shows two tanks; a *Soviet KV-1* and a *German*
Panzerkamptwagon III. Within the stamp image we meet Alexandre Vassilevsky
and a *Soviet T-34 tank*.

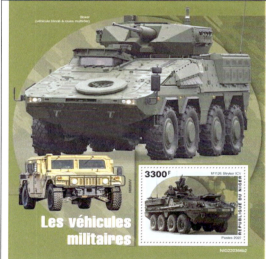

Niger 2022 : Military vehicles including (1) an *American M 113 Troop carrier* in position (3) of the first sheet.

The stamp within the second sheet is a The *BTR-4 "* infantry fighting vehicle designed in Ukraine by the Kharkiv Morozov Machine Building Design Bureau .

The third sheet features the *Boxer* is a multirole armoured fighting vehicle designed by an international consortium to accomplish a number of operations through the use of installable mission modules. Australia uses the *Boxer in its MRAV* (*Multi-Role Armoured Vehicle*) role.

The *M1126 ICV* has a Protector remote weapon station can mount either a .50 calibre M2 or Browning machine gun.

Tanks on stamps

Niger 2022 : The 55th anniversary of the 1967 6-day war.
The tanks depicted on the low-value sheet are (1) Egypt, Syria and Iraq used the *Russian PT-76*, (3) Israel relied upon American vehicles including the AMX-13. The other sheetlet shows the M-51 Super Sherman as the main background, within the stamp the Sherman variant is described as a M-113.

Niuafoʻou

Niuafoʻou is the northernmost island in the kingdom of Tonga. One of the Niua Islands, it is located in the southern Pacific Ocean between Fiji and Samoa. It is a volcanic rim island.

Niuafoʻou 1995 : The 50th Anniversary of End of World War II in the Pacific.
The tank shown is the *M4 Sherman*.

Palau

Palau is an archipelago of over 500 islands, part of the Micronesia region in the western Pacific Ocean.

Palau 2005 : The Route to Victory - The Battle of Kursk.

Palau 1991 : Two stamps from the set of nine; "Operation Desert Storm, Liberation of Kuwait".
The *M2 Bradley tank* and President George H W Bush.

Papua New Guinea

Papua New is a country in Oceania that comprises the eastern half of the island of New Guinea and its offshore islands in Melanesia. Officially the Independent State of Papua New Guinea it shares its only land border with Indonesia to the west and it is directly adjacent to Australia to the south and the Solomon Islands to the east. Its capital, located along its southeastern coast, is Port Moresby. The country is the world's third largest island country.

Tanks on stamps

Papua New Guinea 2011 : World War II Relics.

Image (1) illustrating the relic of a *Japanese 95 Ha Ga tank*.

The Pitcairn Islands

The Pitcairn Islands, officially the Pitcairn, Henderson, Ducie and Oeno Islands, are a group of four volcanic islands in the southern Pacific Ocean that form the sole British Overseas Territory in the Pacific Ocean.

Pitcairn Islands 2010 : "Lest we forget" - The 65th Anniversary of the End of World War II.

One of a set of four stamps. The others show air and Naval images.

Poland

World War II began with the Nazi German invasion of Poland on 1 September 1939, followed by the Soviet invasion of Poland on 17 September. On 28 September 1939, Warsaw fell. As agreed in the Molotov–Ribbentrop Pact, Poland was split into two zones, one occupied by Nazi Germany, the other by the Soviet. A Polish Government in exile was set up in London, 3 issues of stamps.

These three stamps are described on the next page.

Counties of issue – in alphabetical order

- Poland 1941 : Portrayal of Poland in Ruins and the Polish Army in Great Britain (one image from a set of eight) and one image from two other issues. The images are mixed scenes of ruin and warfare.
- Poland 1943 : The Polish Army in Foreign Countries During World War II "Tubruk Road", and
- Poland 1944 : "Monte Cassino" commemoration overprints (one image of four).

Poland 1988 : The 49th anniversary of the outbreak of World War 11 (one image from a set of three).

The personality is named as Bigadier-general Walerian Czuma, for whom data is hard to find.

Poland 2020 : "The Road to Freedom".

One other very colourful issue of 2020 has been the 100th anniversary of the Battle of Warsaw showing hand-to-hand fighting. No armoured vehicles are included amongst the images.

Russia

With massive quantities of weapons and tanks from World War II, and the factories to produce them, the Russians exported hardware and built-up client states which spread their influence and became involved in the continuing state of political conflict, military tension, proxy wars, and economic competition existing afterwards known as the Cold War. (Narration continued on next page).

Tanks on stamps

The Cold War featured periods of relative calm and of international high tension – the Berlin Blockade (1948–1949), the Korean War (1950–1953), the Berlin Crisis of 1961, the Vietnam War (1955–1975), the Cuban Missile Crisis (1962), the Soviet–Afghan War (1979–1989), and various smaller conflicts in which Soviet weapons had significant impact in many wars.

Russia (USSR) 1943 : V V Mayakovsky (50th birthday issue) may have been a poet but the image on these stamps look suspiciously like tanks.

Russia USSR 1943 : "Death to the German invaders " and "Waking the Tiger".

Russia 1945 : Great Fatherland's War, (4 of 6 images from the set).

Russia (USSR) 1945 : "Rear for Front)". The first image represents 'tank production'.

With the onset of the Cold War, the USSR competed with the United States for global ideological influence. The Soviet era of the 20th century saw some of the most significant Russian technological achievements, including the first human-made satellite and the first human expedition into outer space.

Russia (USSR) 1946 : Red Square Parade "Glory to Soviet Tankmen".

Russia (USSR) 1947 : The 29th anniversary of the Soviet Army.

Russia (USSR) 1948 : Tankmans' Day.

Russia (USSR) 1958 : The 40th Anniversary of the Soviet Army.

Tanks on stamps

The fourth stamp (of the set of five) reflects upon the August 1944 death of Vladimir Bogatkin, a Guard Captain of the 1st Separate Anti-tank Artillery Unit of the Army.

Russia (USSR) 1960 : 'Heroes of Second World War' issue. I. D. Chernyakhovsky (1906-1945).

Ivan Chemyakhovsky was the youngest-ever Soviet General of the army. Due to the rapid pre-war expansion of the military and 1937–1938 military purges, he quickly rose in rank. In 1938 he became commander of the 9th Light Tank Brigade. In March 1941 he became the commander of the 28th Tank Division in the Baltic Military District. For his leadership during World War II he was awarded the title Hero of the Soviet Union twice.

Russia (USSR) 1961 : A 'heroes of the Second World War issue'. Sergeant V. P. Miroshnichenko (1916-1941). I cannot add anything – but a tank is crossing a bridge in the image and the date 1941 is shown. Barbarossa?

[1961 : FIRST Manned Space Flight - to add a time reference marker]

Russia (USSR) 1961 : World Youth Forum.

The image seems to show the Youth Forum participants disposing a redundant tank into the sea.

Counties of issue – in alphabetical order

Russia (USSR) 1961 : A 'heroes of the Second World War issue'. One stamp of a set of two.

V S Shalandin (1924-1943). I cannot add any details except that our man appears to be an airman but there are tanks under air attack within the image.

Russia (USSR) 1962 : A 'heroes of the Second World War' issue.
One stamp of a set of four. I V Panfilov (1893-1941) – a controversial hero, a Soviet general and a posthumous Hero of the Soviet Union, known for his command of the 316th Rifle Division during the defence of Moscow.

Russia (USSR) 1963 : The Second World War, the tank Battle of Kursk.

Russia (USSR) 1966 : 25th anniversary of the Battle of Moscow. One of a set of three images; "statue, tank and medal".

The Russian stamp isuing policy from the end of WW2 and until the break-up (1991) of the USSR was non-aggressive. It might be argued that the face showed the world a strategy of "defence of peace". The story told to the world was of Russian space adventure and success. The internal story concentrated upon Lenin, the October Revolution, nationalistic emblems emphasising Socialism,

Tanks on stamps

(continued from last page) - Communism, the Communist Party resolutions and promises (five year plans to be completed in four years). The past war was not emphasised except by regular commemoration of past achievement.

Russia (USSR) 1968 : The 50th Anniversary of Soviet Armed Forces. Two images from a set of 10 and the miniature sheet - these with images of tanks.

Russia USSR 1973 : Background map is of the Battle of Kurst.

Russia (USSR) 1984 : WW2 tanks. (Described on the next page).

The tanks are (1) a medium tank T-34, (2) a heavy tank KV, (3) heavy tank IS-2, (4) a self-propelled gun SU-100 and (5) an ISU-152.

- The *T-34* is a Soviet medium tank from World War II. When introduced, its 76.2 mm tank gun was more powerful than its contemporaries, and its 60-degree sloped armour provided good protection against anti-tank weapons. The T-34 had a profound effect on the conflict on the Eastern Front, and had a long-lasting impact on tank design.
- The *Kliment Voroshilov (KV)* tanks are a series of Soviet heavy tanks named after the Soviet defence commissar and politician Kliment Voroshilov who worked with the Red Army during World War II. The KV tanks were known for their heavy armour protection during the early stages of the war, especially during the first year of the German invasion of the Soviet Union.
- The *IS-2* (Russian: ИС-2, sometimes romanised as JS-2) is a Soviet heavy tank, the second of the IS tank series named after the Soviet leader Joseph Stalin. It was developed and saw combat during World War II and saw service in other Soviet allied countries after the war. Production of the KV-1S was gradually replaced by the SU-152 and ended in April 1943.
- The *SU-100* (*Samokhodnaya Ustanovka* 100) is a Soviet tank destroyer armed with the D-10S 100 mm anti-tank gun in a casemate superstructure. It was used extensively during the last year of World War II and saw service for many years afterwards with the armies of Soviet allies around the world.
- The *ISU-152* with a 152mm calibre gun is a Soviet self-propelled gun developed and used during World War II. It was unofficially nicknamed *Zveroboy* ("beast killer") in response to several large German tanks and guns coming into service, including Tigers and Panthers.

The Russian Federation was formed in 1991 following the collapse of the Communist Party's dominant role in the constitution.

By the mid-1990s Russia had a system of multiparty electoral politics. But it was harder to establish a representative government because of the struggle between president and parliament and the anarchic party system. The central government lost control of the localities, bureaucracy, and economic fiefdoms, and tax revenues had collapsed. Still in a deep depression, Russia's economy was hit further by the financial crash of 1998. At the end of 1999, Yeltsin made a surprise announcement of his resignation, leaving the government in the hands of the Prime Minister Vladimir Putin.

Tanks on stamps

Russia 1993 : The 50ᵗʰ anniversary of the Battle of Kursk.

Russia 1994 : The 50th Anniversary of Liberation of Russia, Belarus and Ukraine. The same image is also used by Belarus but not Ukraine.

Russia 1998 : The 100th Anniversary of the Birth of M.I.Koshkin. Mikhail Koshkin (1898 - 1940) was a Soviet tank designer, chief designer of the famous T-34 medium tank. The T-34 was the most produced tank of World War II. He will again feature on a Russian stamp in 1923.

Russia 2003 : The 60th Anniversary of Battle of Kursk and the 60th Anniversary of the Offensive of the Soviet Army in 1944.

Russia 2005 : 60th Anniversary of Victory in the WWII.

Russia 2005 : Navy Marines (4) the modern sea-infantry of Russia.

Russia 2010 : Tanks - The 65th Anniversary of World War II Victory.
The tanks featured are examined on the next page.

Tanks on stamps

The BT-7M; The BT-7 was the last of the BT series of Soviet cavalry tanks that were produced in large numbers between 1935 and 1940. The BT-7's successor was the famous T-34 medium tank, introduced in 1940, which replaced all of the Soviet fast tanks, infantry tanks, and medium tanks then in service. Designed by Kharkiv Morozov Machine Building Design Bureau (KMDB), a Ukrainian state-owned tank design bureau

(1) The T-70 is a light tank used by the Red Army during World War II, replacing both the T-60 scout tank for reconnaissance. The T-70 was designed by Nicholas Astrov's design team at Factory No. 38 in Kirov.

(2) The Germans also noted that the T-34 was very slow to find and engage targets, while their own tanks could typically get off three rounds for every one fired by the T-34. Due to low anti-tank performance, the T-34 was upgraded to the T-34-85 model. This model, with its 85 mm (3.35 in) ZiS gun, provided greatly increased firepower compared to the previous T-34's 76.2mm gun.

(3) The IS-2 heavy tank, first deliveries were made in October 1943, and the tanks went immediately into service. Production ended in January 1944. Its designation was simplified to IS-1 after the introduction of the IS-122, later renamed as IS-2 for security purposes.

Russia 2010 : 65th anniversary of Victory in WW2. The first of two additional miniature sheets. The sheet featuring the IS-2 has been reduced in size during the scan.

Russia 2010 : 65th anniversary of Victory in WW2. The second additional miniature sheets.

Russia 2014 : The 70th Anniversary of the Liberation of Russia, Belarus and Ukraine.

Russia 2016 : History, centenary of World War I - Military Equipment. Russia had no tanks of its own during WW1, but image (2) certainly shows an armoured vehicle. In 1918 the Red Army established the Soviet of Armoured Units. By 1920 fourteen captured French Renault FT tanks were remanufactured as 'Russkiy Renos', the first Russian tanks.

Tanks on stamps

Russia 2016 : WW2 "The way to victory", the second stamp in the series with a set style, format and colour, the scene is dated 1941 and has the image of a tank. Some issues are joint issues with other administrations.

Russia 2017 : Hero of the Russian Federation. B B Matbeeb. Tank in the background but no other information.

Russia 2018 : WW2 "The way to victory", the eleventh stamp in the series; The Battle of Kursk 1943.

Russia 2018 : WW2 "The way to victory", the fifteenth stamp in the series; The 75th Anniversary of the End of World War II - Joint Issue with Belarus. Dated 1944.

Counties of issue – in alphabetical order

Russia 2019 : "International War Games".

Russia 2020 : WW2 "The way to victory".
The seventeenth and eighteenth stamps in the series; The Vistula-Oder Offensive Operation and the Koenigsberg front. Events dated 1945. This same year the Battles for Berlin and Prague are shown , with military images but these do not reflect the impact of the tank.

Russia 2020 : The 75th Anniversary of the End of World War II - Joint Issue with Belarus. (reduced in the scan).

Tanks on stamps

Russia 2020 : The 100th Anniversary of National Tank Building.

The tanks are described as being (1) T-24), (2) T-26, (3) T-72 and (4) T-14.

(1) The designer has labelled the vehicle as *Borets Za Svobodu Tovarishch Lenin* (*Freedom Fighter Comrade Lenin.* A tank design bureau was established at the Kharkov Locomotive Factory (KhPZ) in Kharkiv, Soviet Ukraine, in 1928. The first tank project of the factory was the T-12 (or T-1-12). The project was re-designated T-24, work was completed fixing problems with the transmission and fuel system, and a larger turret was designed.

(2) The T-26 tank was the Soviet light tank used during many conflicts of the Interwar period and in World War II. It was a development of the British Vickers 6-Ton tank and was one of the most successful tank designs of the 1930s until its light armour became vulnerable to newer anti-tank guns. It was produced in greater numbers than any other tank of the period, with more than 11,000 units manufactured giving it the title of the most produced tank during the interwar period. During the 1930s, the USSR developed 53 variants of the T-26, including flame-throwing tanks, combat engineer vehicles, remotely controlled tanks, self-propelled guns, artillery tractors, and armoured carriers. Twenty-three of these were series-produced, others were experimental models.

(3) The T-72 is a family of Soviet main battle tanks that entered production in 1969. The T-72 was a development based off the T-64 using thought/design of the previous projects. About 25,000 T-72 tanks have been built, and refurbishment has enabled many to remain in service for decades. It has been widely exported and has seen service in 40 countries and in numerous conflicts. The Russian T-90 introduced in 1992 and the Chinese Type 99 are further

developments of the T-72. Production and development of various modernized T-72 models continues today.

(4) The T-14 Armata (is a Russian main battle tank (MBT) based on the Armata Universal Combat Platform. The Russian Army initially planned to acquire 2,300 T-14s between 2015 and 2020. By 2018, production and fiscal shortfalls delayed this to 2025, before Russia announced the apparent cancellation of the main production run on 30 July 2018. However, as of 2021, the Russian state-owned TASS media agency claimed the Armata had been expected to begin serial production in 2022, with delivery of a test batch of 100 to the 2nd Guards Tamanskaya Motor Rifle Division expected to begin in 2022. The tanks are planned to only be officially transferred following completion of all state tests. In December 2021 the Russian state conglomerate Rostec stated that serial production had commenced, with "more than 40" Armata tanks anticipated to be delivered to Russian troops after 2023.

Russia 2021 : Hero of the Russian Federation; Stanislav Morozov.
He was the Commander of the 245th Guards Motor Rifle Regiment, Colonel. A hero, by decree, for courage and heroism displayed during the performance of a special assignment.

Russia 2021 : Technological Achievements.

Tanks on stamps

The image shown in position (3) on the last page is the experimental robotic platform "Marker". This is a joint project of the National Center for the Development of Technologies and Basic Elements of Robotics of the FPI and the NGO "Android Technology". The "Marker" platform can be based on both tracked and wheeled chassis and has a modular architecture. Armament — 7.62 mm machine gun and two anti-tank guided missiles. The "marker" can be paired with a fighter, receiving target designation from the sight of his weapon, or controlled remotely.

Russia 2021 : Tanks.

The tanks are described as being (1) T-34-76, (2) T-54, (3) T-7263 and (4) T-90M.

(1) Based upon the development of the T-34 the two main production models are the T-34/76 and T-34/85 with minor models receiving letter designations such as *T-34/76A*—this nomenclature has been widely used in the west, especially in popular literature.

(2) The T-54 and T-55 tanks are a series of Soviet main battle tanks introduced in the years following the Second World War. The first T-54 prototype was completed at Nizhny Tagil by the end of 1945.[3] From the late 1950s, the T-54 eventually became the main tank for armoured units of the Soviet Army, armies of the Warsaw Pact countries, and many others. T-54s and T-55s have been involved in many of the world's armed conflicts since their introduction in the second half of the 20th century. The T-54/55 series is the most-produced tank in history. Estimated production numbers for the series range from 96,500 to 100,000.

(3) The T-72 is a Soviet-designed main battle tank that entered production in 1971. It replaced the T-54/55 series as the workhorse of Soviet tank

forces (while the T-64 and T-80 served as the Soviet high-technology tanks).[j] In front-line Russian service, T-72s are being upgraded or augmented by the T-90, itself a modernized version of the T-72B. The T-72 has been exported and produced in many countries.

(4) The T-90 is a third-generation Russian main battle tank developed to replace the T-72. It uses a 125 mm 2A46 smoothbore main gun, the 1A45T fire-control system, an upgraded engine, and gunner's thermal sight. Standard protective measures include a blend of steel and composite armour, smoke grenade dischargers, Kontakt-5 explosive reactive armour (ERA) and the Shtora infrared anti-tank guided missile (ATGM) jamming system. The T-90 was designed and built by Uralvagonzavod, in Nizhny Tagil, Russia. It entered service with the Russian army in 1992. The T-90M has been in service since 2016.

Russia 2021 : The 80th anniversary of Victory in the great Patriotic war of 1939-1945 / The uniforms of the Red Army and Navy in 1941.

Russia 2022 : Hero of the Russian Federation.

Igor Grudnov was the Commander of the Eastern District of the National Guard Troops of the Russian Federation. By decree of the President of the Russian Federation of February 29, 2000, for courage and heroism in the elimination of unlawful armed groups in the North Caucasus Region.

Tanks on stamps

Russia 2022 : Heroes of the Russian Federation :

Two stamps from the set of ten – those showing a tank as the background to the subject's valour. Positions (2) and (10) in the set. The Russian names are given in all cases and the date of death – all have died in the Invasion of Ukraine. The postal authority has not followed the issue up with data for the Internet.

Russia 2023 : Hero of the Russian Federation.

N. Kul'kov; the award was for the courage and heroism demonstrated in the performance of military duty in the North Caucasus Region as an Assistant Chief of a Department of the Operational Brigade of internal troops of the Ministry of the Interior of Russia, a Major. Again I only have access the name in Russian script.

Russia 2023 : Heroes of the Russian Federation.

Two stamps from the set of ten – those showing a tank as the background to the subject's valour. Positions (4) and (7) in the set – all have died in the Invasion of Ukraine. 60,000 copies of each image were issued. I am unable to trace any list of those included as 'tank' heroes during the Ukraine War of 2022.

Counties of issue – in alphabetical order

Russia 2023 : Cities of Labor Valor.

I deduce that the city / factory recognised in position (2) is the Research Corporation Ural Wagon Factory located in Nizhny Tagil, Russia. It is one of the largest scientific and industrial complexes in Russia and the largest main battle tank manufacturer in the world.

Russia 2024 : Cities of Military Glory.

Tanks on stamps

São Tomé and Príncipe

São Tomé and Príncipe, an African island nation close to the equator, is part of a volcano chain featuring striking rock and coral formations, rainforests, and beaches. São Tomé and Príncipe gained independence from Portugal in 1975.

São Tomé 2010 : Battles of the Second World War.
In position (4) of sheet 1 Georgy Khukov is shown with a T-34 tank in the background.

São Tomé 2010 : The 60th Anniversary of the Korean War.

São Tomé 2013 : "Pride of France". In Position (3) of sheet 1 De Gaulle is shown with the *Hotchkiss H35/39 military tank*.

São Tomé 2014 : The Second World War. (1) Winston Churchill is shown with what the designer states is a Sherman "Valenciennes" tank in North Africa.

São Tomé 2014 : The 70th anniversary of the Liberation of Paris. General De Gaulle is e dominant personality of this commemoration. He is shown sheet 1 (1) with a Renault tank.

São Tomé 2014 : The 50th anniversary of the death of Winston Churchill. (2) Again WSC is shown with a tank.

Tanks on stamps

São Tomé 2016 : World War II - The 75th Anniversary of the Battle of Moscow. The tank is presumably a T-34 in position (2) within sheet 1.The high value service fee sheet shows General Georgy Zhukov.

In 2018 the São Tomé authority issued a commemoration of the 100th anniversary of WW1 but did not show a tank as an image, but made up for it with the next militaryissue.

São Tomé 2018 : The Battle of Kursk.

The five soldiers recognised, and tanks on the first sheet are (1) Michail Katukov and Nikolai Vatuten with a *Su-52* (2) Walter Model and an *Ilyshin 1I-2;* (3) Ivan Kozhedub and (4) Ivan Konev. The Russian General Georgy Zhukov is shown with a *Pz. Kphe Tiger tank* under fire in the second sheet.

Counties of issue – in alphabetical order

São Tomé 2018 : The 75th anniversary of the Allied Invasion of Sicily.
Bernard Montgomery and Dwight Eisenhower are the two military men shown.
On the sheet one (position 2), the tank is drawn to be a *M4 Sherman tank.*

São Tomé 2018 : The 80th Anniversary of the Beginning of World War II.

The three armoured vehicles in the first sheet are (1) A *Panzerkampfwagon 1*, (3)
The Panzerkampwagon III, and (4) *a TKS tankette.* The image of the
Panzerkampfwagon 1 is repeated on the higher value service fee sheet.

Tanks on stamps

São Tomé 2019 : World War II - The 75th Anniversary of Normandy Landings. The four armoured vehicles in the first sheet are designated (1) a *Semi-lagarta M3*, (2) *a Daimler Dingo*, (3) a Crusader, and (4) an *M8 Greyhound*. The second sheet shows a *Ford GPA* with the *Daimler Dingo* as the main image used as background.

São Tomé 2021 : The 80th Anniversary of the Launching of Operation Barbarossa.

The four tanks shown in the first sheet on the previous page are (1) *Panzer III Ausf. H*, (2) a *KV 2*, (3) *Stug III Ausf.B* and (4) a KV1. The latter two tanks are also shown on the second sheet. Erich von Manstein is the general featured.

Sierra Leone

Sierra Leone, officially the Republic of Sierra Leone, has a unicameral parliament and a directly elected president. It is a country on the southwest coast of West Africa. It shares its southeastern border with Liberia, and the northern half of the nation is surrounded by Guinea.

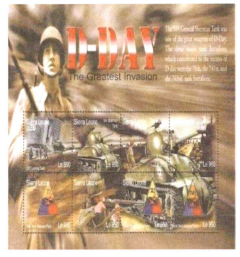 

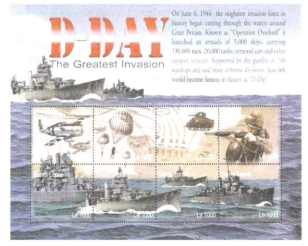

Sierra Leone 2004 :

The 60th Anniversary of D-Day Landings.

3 of the six miniature sheets in the single issue. (48 images of the invasion).

The tanks illustrated here are the *M4 Sherman*.

General Montgomery and Dwight Eisenhower are shown on the sixth image

Sierra Leone 2005 : The 60th Anniversary of the Ending of World War II.
Eight miniature sheets were issued in the single issue
One sheet specifically looks at the Battle of Stalingrad.
Other sheets are people oriented and the final two images recognise VE and VJ events.

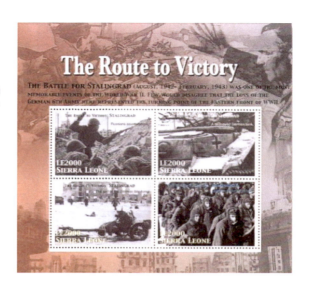

Sierra Leone 2015 : World War II - The 70th Anniversary of the End of the Second World War.

The context of (1) image of sheet 1 is the Battle of Berlin in 1945, and an *ISU-52 Russian Tank.*

Sierra Leone 2015 : Military transport.

Within sheet one (2*) Leopard 2*, developed by Krauss-Maffei in the 1970s, the tank entered service in 1979 and replaced the *Leopard 2E*. Within sheet 2 the background features the *M1A2 Abrams tank*.

Sierra Leone 2015 : The 40th anniversary of the end of the Vietnam War. Within sheet two the tank looks like the *M8 Patten*.

Tanks on stamps

Sierra Leone World War II – Dogs and tanks. (What an eclectic mix from the postal authority).

The tanks illustrated within sheet one are (1) *US M14 Chaffee*, (2) German *Tiger 1*, (3) Russian *Su-122,* (4) *Tiger 1* and the second sheet background is made up of another *Tiger 1* and within the actual stamp image a *US medium M3 tank*.

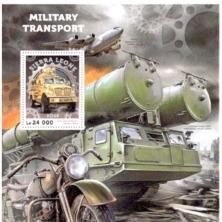

Sierra Leone 2016 : Transportation - Military Transport.

Sheet one (3) shows an M1128 Wolfpack mobile gun system. The M1128 MGS is fitted with a 105mm M68 gun, which has similar firepower to the M60 main battle tank gun. Armour plating provides protection from autocannon fire.

Sierra Leone 2016 : World War II - the 75th anniversary of the Battle of Moscow. Within the first sheet (3) represents a *Panzer IV* whilst the contextual background pits a *Russian T-34* against a *Panzer III. (4)* German general Heinz Guderian is pictured. Russian general Georgy Zhukov is shown on both sheets.

Sierra Leone 2017 : The 100th Anniversary of Russian Revolution. Perhaps stretching the tank theme a bit too far these two sheets include images of Lenin (1) and (3) also includes Nadezhda Krupskaya who was the secretary of the Central Committee of the Bolshevik Party during the revolution of 1905, and served as the deputy commissar of education following the October Revolution. Tzar Nickolas II is also shown in sheet one. The Tzar and Lenin also appear in sheet two with the stamp showing a *Nakashidze-Charron M1906 armoured car.*

Tanks on stamps

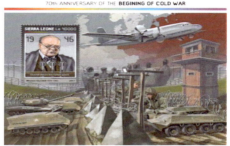

Sierra Leone 2017 : The 70th anniversary of the beginning of the Cold War. Within the background US armour (*M48 Patton* and a *US Army M35 Tank destroyer*) are aligned up against an unknown Russian tank destroyer.

Sierra Leone 2017 : The 75th anniversary of the Battle of Stalingrad. A *Russian T-34* enters the city while at (3) the main image within the second sheet the patriot confronts the German aggressor.

Sierra Leone 2018 : The Battle of Moscow
Again featured are the T-34 tank and Marshal Georgy Zhukov.

Sierra Leone 2018 The 100th anniversary of the end of WW1.
The tanks shown within sheet one are (2) The Renault FT and (3) A Mark IV.

Tanks on stamps

Sierra Leone 2019 : The Battle of Kursk. Four stamps and a miniature sheet. The tanks shown in sheet one are (1) *Russian Panther tank* and (4) *German Tiger 1 heavy tank*. Georgy Khukov is the featured commander with a Panther tank as the background to the portrait.

Sierra Leone 2019 : The 75th anniversary of the Normandy Landings. The tank shown in sheet one (3) is the *M4 Sherman*.

Sierra Leone 2019 : The 145th Anniversary of the Birth of Sir Winston Churchill, 1874-1965.

The tank within sheet one (3) is labelled a (German) *Tiger 131.*

Sierra Leone 2019 : The 70th Anniversary of the People's Republic of China. I believe the tank illustrated is the Type 99 or ZTZ-99, a Chinese third generation main battle tank.

Tanks on stamps

Sierra Leone 2019 : The 105th anniversary of the beginning of WW1.
The tanks shown, sheet one (3) are a *British Mark 1* and (4) a *German Empire tank AV7.*

Sierra Leone 2019 : The 1944 Battle of the Bulge.
The tanks illustrated within sheet one are : (1) A *German Sturmgeschütz armoured vehicle*, (2) A *Cromwell Mk VIII*, (3) A *Churchill Mk IV* and (4) *M4 Sherman*. The designer calls the German tank destroyer image on the second sheet a *Jagdtiger* whilst the background shows the *Churchill Mk IV* – the third repeated image of the lower service fee sheet of four.

Sierra Leone 2020 : Battle of Iwo Jima. Sheet one (1) *a Japanese Chi-Ha medium tank*.

Sierra Leone 2020 : The 75th anniversary of the Yalta Conference. The tank shown is a *Russian T-34-85.*

Sierra Leone 2022 : The 80th Anniversary of the End of the Battle of Moscow.

The soldier recognised in the lower value sheet is Aleksandr Mikhaylovich Vasilevsky, a Soviet career-officer in the Red Army who attained the rank of Marshal of the Soviet Union in 1943. He served as the Chief of the General Staff of the Soviet Armed Forces. The other portrait is of Georgy Khukov.

The tanks shown on the Battle of Moscow images are (1) ISU-122, used as a powerful assault gun, a self-propelled howitzer, and a long-range tank destroyer (2) T-34, (3) SU-76 a Soviet light self-propelled gun and (4) SU-85. The "SU" abbreviation stands for "Samokhoknaya Ustanovka" which means "self-propelled gun" and the 85 stands for the 85mm D-5T gun. The SU-85 had a crew of four men. Despite the fact that the SU-85 was a self-propelled gun, it was worthy of the title tank destroyer. The designer has added the note textually that the SU tanks "were actually produced after the battle". Both the stamp and the background of the Khukov sheet show the T-34 in action.

Sierra Leone 2022 : The 80th anniversary of the ending of the Battle of Moscow.
During the early 2020s Sierra Leone started to issue three miniature sheets each issue. The stamp image is a *Panzer IV* was the most numerous German tank. The background image is a Russian SU-76.

105 years since the Battle of Arras

SRL220144a

Sierra Leone 2022 : 105th year anniversary of the Battle of Arras, WW1.

I shall only reproduce one of three miniature sheets. The other two concentrate upon air activity and feature portraits of Julian Bing, the Canadian commander, and Erich Ludendorff of Germany.

On this sheet featured are Manfred von Richthoven and the British *Mark IV tank*.

Sierra Leone 2022 : "70 years since the Battle of Triangle Hill", Korea.
One miniature sheet of three featuring a *Russian T-34*.
The main combatants were two United Nations (UN) infantry divisions, with additional support from the United States Air Force, against elements of the Chinese People's Volunteer Army (PVA) 15th and 12th Corps.
The battle was part of UN attempts to gain control of the "Iron Triangle" and took place from 14 October to 25 November 1952.

Tanks on stamps

Sierra Leone 2022 : Chinese art. One of five miniature sheets with this title.

After the signing of Sino-Soviet Treaty of Friendship, Alliance, and Mutual Assistance, the Soviets agreed to assist China in building a tank manufacturing facility to manufacture the T-54, a MBT in 1956. Initially, the tanks were assembled with Soviet-supplied parts, which were gradually replaced by Chinese-made components. The tank was accepted into service by the PLA in 1959, and given the designation *Type 59*. I believe the designer has based his image upon the *Type 59 tank*.

Singapore

Singapore 1977 : 10th anniversary of National Service.

Singapore 1987 : 20th anniversary of National Service.

Singapore, as expected did celebrate the 50th anniversary of National service in 2017 but did not use images of military equipment. Portraits of leaders from 1967, Lee Kwan Yew and Goh Keng Swee were used.

Solomon Islands

Solomon Islands is a country consisting of six major islands and over 900 smaller islands in Melanesia, part of Oceania, to the northeast of Australia. The Solomon Islands has been a prolific issuer of postage stamps, (through its appointed Postal Administration Agent). The *Stampworld* catalogue records stamp issues from 1907 to 2017. A search of Ebay suggests the country has found disfavour from the distribution companies.

Solomon Islands 2014 : The 70th anniversary of the Battle of the Bulge. The tank images used in the first sheet are (1) *the German Panther*, (2) *an US Light tank* , (3) *The M7 Priest* - The 105 mm Howitzer Motor Carriage M7 was an American self-propelled gun vehicle produced during World War II. It was given the official service name 105 mm Self Propelled Gun, Priest by the British Army, due to the pulpit-like machine gun ring, and following on from the Bishop and the contemporary Deacon self-propelled guns. The second sheet shows an *M4 Sherman*.

Tanks on stamps

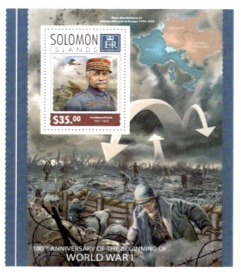

Solomon Islands 2014 : The 100th anniversary of the beginning of WW1. These two miniature sheets concentrate upon leaders of the time. Sheet one portrays (1) King Albert of Belgium, (2) Joesph Joffre, (3) Theobald von Bethmann-Hollweg, and (4) Franz Ferdinand of Austria. Through the high service fee sheet we meet Ferdinand Foch. The tank within the first sheet appears to be a *Mark 1*.

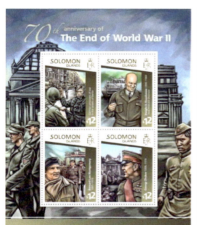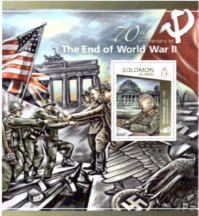

Solomon Islands 2015 : The 70th anniversary of the end of WW2. A similar two sheet format. The personalities are (2) Dwight D Eisenhower, (3) Bernard Montgomery and (4) Georgy Khukov. The tank, background to the Eisenhower portrait is a Sherman Tank M4A6. The final portrait shows Field Marshall Willhelm Keitel.

Solomon Islands 2015 : The 70th anniversary of the liberation of Auschwitz. The tanks in sheet one are both T-34s. The portrait is of Oskar Schindler, a German industrialist, humanitarian and member of the Nazi Party who is credited with saving the lives of 1,200 Jews during the Holocaust by employing them in his enamelware and ammunitions factories in occupied Poland and the Protectorate of Bohemia and Moravia.

Solomon Islands 2016 : The 75th anniversary of the Battle of Moscow. The three soldiers shown are Fedor von Bock, Alexandr Vasilevsky and Georgy Khukov. The two tanks featured are from the German Third Panzer Army and a *Russian T-34*.

Tanks on stamps

Solomon Islands 2017 : "Special transport" – the second of two miniature sheets.

This image shows the *Bushmaster Infantry Mobility Vehicle,* an Australian-built four-wheel drive armoured vehicle. The Bushmaster was primarily designed by the then government-owned Australian Defence Industries (ADI). It is in service in several country armies.

Solomon Islands 2017 : Charles de Gaulle (1890-1970).
Sheet one includes the image of a French Char B1 with the General.

Counties of issue – in alphabetical order

South Africa

South Africa 1941 : War effort, bilingual text.

 South Africa 1942 : War effort, half-size images.

The republic of South Africa was established in 1961.

Tanks on stamps

St Helena

Saint Helena is one of the three constituent parts of Saint Helena, Ascension and Tristan da Cunha, a British overseas territory located in the South Atlantic Ocean. Saint Helena is a remote volcanic tropical island 1,950 km (1,210 mi) west of the coast of south-western Africa, and 4,000 km (2,500 mi) east of Rio de Janeiro in South America.

St Helena 2005 : The 60th Anniversary of the End of the Second World War. One stamp from a set of ten with mixed themes. It shows the *Churchill Infantry tank*.

St Kitts

St. Kitts is the larger of the 2 Caribbean islands that comprise the nation of Saint Kitts and Nevis. It's known for rain forested mountains and beaches of white, grey, and black sands. On its southwestern coast is the capital, Basseterre, and Georgian buildings from the colonial era. Anchoring Basseterre is the Circus, a plaza modelled after London's Piccadilly Circus, complete with Victorian-style clock tower.

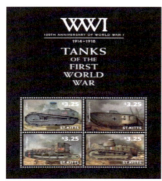 

St Kitts 2014 : Tanks of WW1. Sheet 1 includes (1) *The US M1917*, (2), (3) *British Mark IV* and (4) the *French Renault FT-17*. On the second sheet are (1) *The British Mark IV* and (2) *the German A7V*.

St Vincent

St. Vincent and the Grenadines is a southern Caribbean nation comprising a main island, St. Vincent, and a chain of smaller islands.

St Vincent 1990 : History of the Second World War. Single image from a set of 10. (3) The Narrative reads "British drive Italian Army out of Egypt".

St Vincent and the Grenadines 1995 : The 50th Anniversary of the End of World War II.

The main contextual image shows the entrance to Auschwitz Camp in 1945. Of the eight stamps within the sheet three show images of tanks.

Tanks on stamps

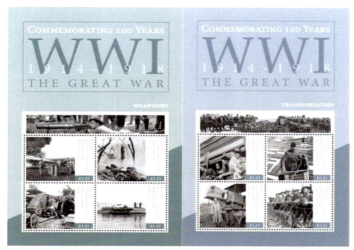

St Vincents – Mayreau 2014 : The 100th Anniversary of the Beginning of World War I.

Two sheets of four. The other two sheets follow on the next page.

St Vincents – Mayreau 2014 : The 100th Anniversary of the Beginning of World War I.

Two sheets associated with issue on the last page., 10 stamp images two sub-headings; "Weaponry" and "Transportation". The background image of a burnt-out *Mark 1 tank* warns of the realities of warfare.

St Vincent – Mustique 2015 World War I - The 2nd Battle of the Marne, 1918. The two leaders shown are Erich Ludendorff and Ferdinand Foch. The image used in the second, smaller miniature sheet, is taken from a photograph that claims to show captured *British Mark IV tanks.*

St Vincent and the Grenadines 2000 : "The World at War" #1. The two tanks (3) *Soviet T-34 Panzer* and (8) *M113 Panzer*.

St Vincent and the Grenadines 2000 : "The World at War" #2.
The three tanks (2) Soviet T-72 Panzer (4) *Soviet M-48 Panzer* and (8) *M-1-A Panzer*.

St Vincent and the Grenadines : 2020 Vietnam War - U.S. Marines.
Sheet one, position (1) illustrates Operation Starlit (1965) (also known in Vietnam as Battle of Van Tuong) was the first major offensive action conducted by a purely U.S. military unit during the Vietnam War from 18 to 24 August 1965. The tank is a *M48 Patton* tank.

Tajikistan

Tajikistan, officially the Republic of Tajikistan, is a landlocked country in Central Asia. Dushanbe is the capital and most populous city. Tajikistan is bordered by Afghanistan to the south, Uzbekistan to the west, Kyrgyzstan to the north, and China to the east. It is separated from Pakistan by Afghanistan's Wakhan Corridor.

Tajikistan 2020 : The 75th Anniversary of the End of World War II.
Three images from a mixed set of 8 war images. (3) Showing a Russian T-34 Tank confronting a *German Panther VI Ausf. E.* (6) A *German P : Kpfw V Panther* and a *US M4A3 Sherman tank* and (7) *Russian T-34-85 tanks.*

Togo

Togo, (officially the Togolese Republic), is a country in West Africa. It is bordered by Ghana to the west, Benin to the east and Burkina Faso to the north. It is one of the least developed countries. Togo has been a prolific issuer of postage stamps, (through its appointed Postal Administration Agent). The *Stampworld* catalogue records stamp issues from 1914 to 2018. A search of Ebay suggests the country may have prejudiced its relationship with the on-line retailer

Togo 2016 : The 100th Anniversary of the First Use of Tanks in Battle.

In logical order the images show a *French Schneider CA1*, a *British Mark IV*, another *Mark IV*, and a *French Saint-Chamond.* The high service fee sheet illustrates the *GB Mark 1* and a *German A7V.* The background, again, shows the *Mark IV.*

Togo 2016 : The 75th anniversary of the Battle of Moscow.
A *German Panzer IV* tank is shown in position 3 of sheet one, and also in sheet two confronting a *Russian T-34/76*.

Togo 2018 : The 100th anniversary of the end of WW1.
Five leaders are shown across the two sheets; General Foch, King Albert of Austria, General Haig and *Mark 1 tank*, Marshall Petain and US General Pershing with the *Mark IV tank* dominating the background.

Togo 2018 : World War II - Battle of Stalingrad.

The two opposing Stalingrad generals are featured on these two miniature sheets; General Paulus and General Joukov. The tank shown is the *German Panzerkampfwagen IV.*

Togo 2019 : The 80th anniversary of the beginning of WW2.

The two diplomats who headline this issue are Russia's Molotov and Germany's von Ribbentrop – the non-aggression agreement broken by Germany in 1941 with Operation Barbarossa. The German Officer is General Fedo von Bock. The two tanks shown are a *Panzer II* and the *7TP* (Siedmiotonowy polski - 7-tonne) Polish light *tank*. It was developed from the British Vickers 6-ton tank.

Tuvalu

Tuvalu, formerly known as the Ellice Islands, is an island country in the Polynesian subregion of Oceania in the Pacific Ocean, about midway between Hawaii and Australia. It lies east-northeast of the Santa Cruz Islands (which belong to the Solomon Islands), northeast of Vanuatu, southeast of Nauru, south of Kiribati, west of Tokelau, northwest of Samoa and Wallis and Futuna, and north of Fiji.

IPGC have chosen a 1967-1969 location / confrontation "the Hill of Angels" to commemorate the Vietnam War and an image of the tanks in use at the time.

Tanks on stamps

Tuvalu 2007 : The Hill of Angels. Miniature sheet #1.

Con Thien (meaning the "Hill of Angels") was a military base that started out as a U.S. Army Special Forces camp before transitioning to a United States Marine Corps combat base. It was located near the Vietnamese Demilitarized Zone (DMZ) about 3 kilometres (1.9 mi) from North Vietnam in Gio Linh District, Quảng Trị Province. It was the site of fierce fighting from February 1967 through February 1968.

Four facets of the fighting are shown on the lower values miniature sheet :
- Marines on patrol,
- Operation Kingfisher took place from 16 July to 31 October 1967,
- Operation Kentucky took place from 1 November 1967 to 28 February 1969 and resulted in 520 Marines killed and 2698 wounded, while US reports claim the PAVN lost 3,839 killed, 117 captured and an unknown number wounded.
- Operation Hickory II. Following the conclusion of Operation Buffalo, III MAF ordered a sweep of the southern half of the DMZ. Operation Hickory II lasted from 14–16 July and resulted in 39 PAVN killed for the loss of 4 Marines dead and 90 wounded.

During July the Army transferred Con Thien to the Marines.

Tuvalu 2008 : US Tanks of the Vietnam War.

The four US tanks shown within the miniature sheet are :

The M60 is an American second-generation main battle tank. It was officially standardized as the Tank, Combat, Full Tracked: 105-mm Gun, M60 in March 1959.

The M551 "Sheridan" AR/AAV was a light tank developed by the United States and named after General Philip Sheridan, of American Civil War fame. It was designed to be landed by parachute and to swim across rivers.

The M113 is a fully tracked armoured personnel carrier that was developed and produced by the Food Machinery and Chemical Corporation.

The Flame Thrower Tank M67 is an American medium flame tank that was briefly used by the U.S. Army, and later by the U.S. Marine Corps during the Vietnam War. Nic-named the "Zippo".

The action photograph / background to the miniature sheet shows a *M48 Patton and M113 AcAvs*.

Tanks on stamps

Tuvalu 2017 : World War ii, 70th anniversary.

One of two miniature sheets, Kokoda Trail photographs in a contextual background. This example projects the tank as a weapon.

Uganda

Uganda, officially the Republic of Uganda, is a landlocked country in East Africa. The country is bordered to the east by Kenya, to the north by South Sudan, to the west by the Democratic Republic of the Congo, to the south-west by Rwanda, and to the south by Tanzania.

Uganda 1990 : The 50th Anniversary of Second World War.

Three images from the set of ten. Personalities featured in the set include General De Gaulle and Douglas MacArthur in addition to (1) early Allies' vehicles, (3) US forces and (9) is labelled the first Battle of El Alamein.

Uganda 1995 : The 50th Anniversary of End of Second World War in Europe. Images (2) and (6) suggests the advance to which tanks have contributed, presumably *Russian T-34s*.

Ukraine

Until recently I have little or no experience with Ukraine stamps although the postal authority has issues stamps from 1918. Looking through issues I get the impression, not of oppression, but a whimsical approach to the images used, prior to the 2022 war, and that includes Ukraine history.

Ukraine 1994 : The 50th Anniversary of Liberation of Russia, Ukraine and Belarus.

Tanks on stamps

Ukraine 2005 : The 50th anniversary of the end of WW2. Included for interest.

Ukraine 2016 : Military vehicles. I presume these are derivatives of Russian tanks.

Ukraine 2017 : Military vehicles.

In 2018 the Ukrainian authority continued with a military theme – this year "ground forces". No issue in 2019.

Ukraine 2020 : National Military equipment.

Counties of issue – in alphabetical order

Ukraine 2021 : Armed Forces of the Ukraine - Land Forces.
(An early warning by the 'government' of a pending problem?)

The Russian Invasion – February 2022

Ukraine 2022 : Ukrainian Tractor Towing Destroyed Russian Tank.
Perhaps one of the most famous images of recent times.

Ukraine 2022 : "Free, Unbreakable, Invincible".

Ukraine 2022 : Ukraine weaponry.

Ukraine 2023 : Hero cities of Ukraine.

In addition to renewing the status of Kyiv, Odesa, Sevastopol and Kerch, decree 111 also awarded the title to the cities;

Chernihiv, Hostomel, Kharkiv, Kherson, Mariupol and Volnovakha. On March 25, 2022, Zelenskyy gave the title of Hero City to another 4 cities by decree No. 164/2022, namely: Bucha, Irpin, Okhtyrka and Mykolaiv.

Counties of issue – in alphabetical order

Ukraine 2023 : Tribute to the Security Forces of Ukraine.

Ukraine 2023 : Main Directorate of Intelligence of the Ministry of Defence and Tribute to Ukraine Security Services.

Ukraine 2023 : Weapons of Victory - The World with Ukraine.
The current conflict opposes the US built Abram tank with latest Russian T-90M, with reports on the superiority of the Abrams.

Tanks on stamps

Ukraine 2024 : Ukrposhta by Your Side.

United States

United States 1953 : George C Patton.

United States 1991 : "A world at war". Miniature sheet.

Counties of issue – in alphabetical order

The usually conservative US Postal Service issued a series of 5 miniature sheets, # 1, 1941 is shown above. To the left are shown the two tank images from the complete set of 50 images within the issue commemorating World War II.

United States 1991 : "USA becomes "arsenal of democracy".

 United States 2003 : The Korean War.

Vietnam

Vietnam 1976 : Liberation of South Vietnam.

Vietnam 1984 : One of the set of seven "The 40th Anniversary of Vietnamese People's Army".

Tanks on stamps

Vietnam 2007 : The 100th Birth Anniversaries of Le Duan.

Lê Duẩn (1907- 1986) was a Vietnamese communist politician. He rose in the party hierarchy in the late 1950s and became General Secretary of the Central Committee of the Communist Party of Vietnam (VCP) at the 3rd National Congress in 1960. He continued Hồ Chí Minh's policy of ruling through collective leadership. From the mid-1960s (when Hồ's health was failing) until his own death in 1986, he was the top decision-maker in Vietnam.

The Battle of Kursk

The Battle of Kursk was a major World War II Eastern Front battle between the forces of Germany and the Soviet Union near Kursk in southwestern Russia during the summer of 1943; it ultimately became the largest tank battle in history and resulted in a Soviet victory. It is considered by some to be the turning point of the European theatre of war instead of the Battle of Stalingrad several months earlier.

The battle began with the launch of the German offensive Operation Citadel , on 5 July, which had the objective of pinching off the Kursk salient with attacks on the base of the salient from north and south simultaneously. After the German offensive stalled on the northern side of the salient, on 12 July the Soviets commenced their Kursk Strategic Offensive Operation with the launch of Operation Kutuzov against the rear of the German forces on the same side. On the southern side, the Soviets also launched powerful counterattacks the same day, one of which led to a large armoured clash, the Battle of Prokhorovka. On 3 August, the Soviets began the second phase of the Kursk Strategic Offensive Operation with the launch of Operation Polkovodets Rumyantsev against the German forces on the southern side of the salient.

The Germans hoped to weaken the Soviet offensive potential for the summer of 1943 by cutting off and enveloping the forces that they anticipated would be in the Kursk salient. Hitler believed that a victory here would reassert German strength and improve his prestige with his allies, who he thought were considering withdrawing from the war. It was also hoped that large numbers of Soviet prisoners would be captured to be used as slave labour in the German armaments industry. The Soviet government had foreknowledge of the German intentions, provided in part by British intelligence's Tunny intercepts. Aware months in advance that the attack would fall on the neck of the Kursk salient, the Soviets built a defence in depth designed to wear down the German armoured spearhead. The Germans delayed the offensive while they tried to build up their forces and waited for new weapons, giving the Red Army time to construct a series of deep defensive belts and establish a large reserve force for counter-offensives.

The battle was the final strategic offensive that the Germans were able to launch on the Eastern Front. Because the Allied invasion of Sicily began during the battle, Adolf Hitler was forced to divert troops training in France to meet the Allied threat in the Mediterranean, rather than using them as a strategic reserve for the Eastern Front. Hitler cancelled the offensive at Kursk after only a week, in part to divert forces to Italy. Germany's extensive losses of men and tanks ensured that the victorious Soviet Red Army enjoyed the strategic initiative for the remainder of the war. The Battle of Kursk was the first time in the Second World War that a German strategic offensive was halted before it could break through enemy defences and penetrate to its strategic depths. Though the Red Army had succeeded in winter offensives previously, their counter-offensives after the German attack at Kursk were their first successful summer offensives of the war.

An expert's assessment of the Russian tank situation in 2024

Russia could run out of infantry fighting vehicles in two or three years, if a recent assessment is accurate. It might run out of tanks around the same time.

According to one count, the Russian armed forces went to war in Ukraine in February 2022 with 2,987 tanks. After 23 months of hard fighting, the Russians have lost at least 2,619 tanks that independent analysts can confirm.

That's 1,725 destroyed, 145 damaged, 205 abandoned and 544 captured T-55s, T-62s, T-72s, T-80s and T-90s.

If the Kremlin didn't have options for replacing war losses, the Russian military would be down to just 368 tanks: far too few to defend against Ukraine's own armour corps, which between pre-war tanks, restored tanks and donated tanks—minus losses—might number around a thousand vehicles.

But the Kremlin *does* have sources of replacement tanks: the Uralvagonzavod factory in southern Russia, which manufactures new T-90Ms, plus four other facilities that repair and modernize old tanks that have been mouldering in storage. Some for decades.

The big question—one that no outside analyst definitively has answered—is how many tanks Uralvagonzavod can *build*, and how tanks the other plants can *repair*.

The Kremlin claims it received 1,500 new and modernized tanks following an intensive industrial effort that roughly tripled vehicle-generation in 2023. If that's true—a big if—it would be reasonable to assume the Russian armed forces received around 500 new and modernized tanks in 2022 (David Axe, 2024).

Counties of issue – in alphabetical order

Notes :

1) **Sources :** As a stamp collector I have many of the relevant stamp images within my collection that I have scanned to obtain the digital image.

a. Stamp collectors are a funny bunch. We mostly start collecting at a young age and accumulate all / any stamps we can find. But with maturity, and because the postal authorities currently issue too many stamps we are obliged to specialise upon specific countries or themes.

b. What we collect is a matter of self-determination. In my case, I expect to collect all the issues, recognised as pre-payment for legitimate post office services for the countries of my interest.

c. Catalogues that list a retailer's selling price for stamps vary in accord with the integrity and or specialisation of the list. For example, The Campbell Paterson of New Zealand Stamps records whether the stamp has been printed on paper with a vertical or horizontal mesh, which involves knowing how paper is made.

d. Postage stamps are usually printed on sheets containing stamps of the same value, the pre-paid service fee. Two stamps joined together by the perforation, if of different values are of interest to the collector.

e. Miniature sheets include stamp images within an enlarged print area to add contextual details that explain the message that the designer wants to tell. It may include details of the image.

f. Stamps sold for everyday use are known as definitive issues and may be on sale for a number of years. The clerk in the post office will offer a definitive stamp as their first choice for the customer.

g. Stamps that are issued to raise specific awareness, such as an anniversary or event are known as 'special issues' and will be on sale for only six months. The customer may need to ask to buy stamps from the special issue.

h. Since the 1990s the context and reason for the issue within the stamp image has been increased to interest theme collectors – such as within this study – the Vietnam War.

i. Stamps may also interest 'souvenir-hunters' of events and specific themes.

j. Stamps are additionally marketed by the postal authority as a first day cover, issue posted on that date and are a respected revenue source for the authority.

k. The pre-payment of the service is cancelled when the stamp is affixed to an addressed piece of mail and submitted to the postal service by submission through a post office remote collection point, (a letterbox on the street), or directly over the counter in a post office.

l. The cancellation is usually made with an inked postmark applied mechanically or by hand by the post office to show the date and the place from which that the item was accepted by the post office as pre-payment of the relevant fee for service. Fees vary dependent upon the service required.

m. A stamp that has been acquired to prepay a service fee but not used for purpose is classified as being in 'mint' condition. A stamp that has been 'used', cancelled by the receiving post office is designated as such. My preference is to collect stamps that have been used, and I place an extra value upon them if they clearly show a cancellation including date and starting location.

n. I have additionally used digital images of stamps available through the Internet from stamp dealers such as <stampworld.com>, a retail organisation based in Europe. 'E-bay' is also a reliable source of data as to what stamps have been issued. These retail sources are most comprehensive.

2) My objective has been to describe the images published by the world's postal authorities to commemorate the effect of tanks during wars. I have scanned and reproduced these images country by country. I believe this is accurate to within 15%. Discrepancies occur, for example, when the image is used more than once by the authority. An image might well be issued with a gummed backing and well as a self-adhesive item. To my mind they are the one image and counted as one. Using the same image in different formats is quite common with the commemorative issues we are looking at. The individual stamp image will appear as a single stamp within a set of stamps, as part of a miniature sheet when the set is shown in its entirety and used in a Prestige Stamp booklet, where the stamps and their representation are described in detail.

3) Postal authorities differentiate between special stamps, the sort of commemoration events we are discussing, and definitive stamps. Definitive stamps, also described as 'everyday stamps, may use the same image on a stamp for as many as 50 years, as is the case of the portrait of Queen Elizabeth II, on Great Britain stamps. Service fee values change but not the image. Special stamps are only available for sale in a country's post offices for 6 months to one year.

4) Where a set of stamps has also been included within a miniature sheet I have scanned and included the latter where possible to enhance the message by including the context.

5) This analysis has left me with several avenues of military history to pursue.

6) I have enjoyed working on my own stamp collection and for this. I trust I have been able to convey that sense of satisfaction to my readers.

Christopher B. Yardley.
Cannava@iinet.net.au
May 2024.

Counties of issue – in alphabetical order

References

David Axe (10.i.24) Forbes
(https://www.forbes.com/sites/davidaxe/2024/01/10/russia-might-be-running-out-of-tanks/?sh=1524cac51027. Downloaded 12.ii.24.

Yardley, Christopher B (2017), A quiet and efficient Captain of Aircraft. Canberra, The Military Historical Society of Australia : ISBN 978-0-6480-9020-5.

Yardley, Christopher B (2019), A Great War Study – The Centenary commemorative postage stamps 2014-2018, Canberra, Cannava House Publications. ISBN 978-0-6486-6710-0.

Yardley, Christopher B (2022), The Second World War – representing world conflict on postage stamps, Canberra, Cannaver House Publications / Balboa Press. Volume One ISBN 978-1-9822-9297-3.
Volume Two ISBN 978-1-9822-9299-7.

Yardley, Christopher B (2022), Other Wars of the Twentieth Century- Stories told through postage stamps, Cannaver House Publications / Balboa Press. ISBN 978-1-9822-9594-3.

Brown, J. (2014). *Anzac's long shadow*. Collingwood, Victoria: Black Inc.

Klacisz, Mateusz. (2015). Visual Propaganda in the Democratic Republic of Afganistan. *Polish Journal of Arts and Culture #14.*

Raento and Brunn. (2005). Visualising Finland : Postage stamps as political messengers. *Geografiska Annaler Series B, Volume 87*(Issue 2), 145-163.

Shelley, Ronald G. (1967). *The postal history of the Spanish Civil War, 1936-1939.* Brighton: R.G. Shelley, 1967.

Wellington, J. (2017). *Exhibiting war : The Great War, museums and memory in Britain, Canada and Australia*. Cambridge, UK: Cambridge University Press.

Budget 2015, *Honest History Factsheet, Honest History website, Accessed 2024.*

Collections of Australian Stamps Melbourne, Australia Post.

Tanks on stamps

New Zealand Stories in Stamps, Wellington, New Zealand.
Royal Mail Special Stamps, London, UK.

Stanley Gibbons (Country) catalogues, Ringwood, UK.
Yvert & Tellier Catalogue des Timbre-poste de France, Amiens, France.
The Michel Katalog of Schwaneberger Verlag Gmbh of Germany.
The *Scott Standard Stamp Catalogue* of the USA.

Google and Wikipedia for basic confirmation of names, places and events
described within stamp images.

_____

Milton Keynes UK
Ingram Content Group UK Ltd.
UKRC030224030824
446459UK00006B/32